Beyond Belief

Josh Hamilton

WITH TIM KEOWN

Beyond Belief

FINDING THE STRENGTH TO COME BACK

New York   Boston   Nashville

The names and identifying characteristics of some characters and places in this book have been changed. However, all the stories herein are true.

Faith Words
Hachette Book Group
237 Park Avenue
New York, NY 10017

Visit our Web site at www.HachetteBookGroup.com

Faith Words is a division of Hachette Book Group, Inc.
The Faith Words name and logo are trademarks of Hachette Book Group, Inc.

Library of Congress Cataloging-in-Publication Data

Hamilton, Josh
Beyond belief : finding the strength to come back / Josh Hamilton — 1st ed.
p. cm.
Summary: "Josh Hamilton chronicles his comeback from drug and alcohol addiction to playing baseball in the major leagues" — Provided by the publisher
ISBN-13: 978-1-59995-161-4
1. Hamilton, Josh, 1981– 2. Baseball players — United States — Biography. 3. Texas Rangers (Baseball team) — Biography. 4. Recovering addicts — United States — Biography. 5. Substance abuse — Religious aspects — Christianity — Case studies. 6. Spiritual life — Christianity — Case studies. 7. Hamilton, Josh, 1981 — Family. 8. Raleigh (N.C.) — Biography. I. Title.
GV865.H24A3 2008
796.357092 — dc22
[B]
2008033708

Printed in the United States of America

First Edition: October 2008

10 9 8 7 6 5 4 3 2 1

This book is dedicated to my beautiful wife, Katie:
For your unconditional love and support. You are an
amazing wife, mother, and friend. I love you.

ACKNOWLEDGMENTS

First and foremost, I'd like to thank my Lord and Savior, Jesus Christ for never leaving my side through the storms. Also for allowing me to have this platform so I can share the Message of Jesus, The Way, The Truth, and The Light.

To my wife: Katie, thank you for always being by my side through the tough times and the good. I thank you for my beautiful children: Julia, Sierra, and Michaela. I love you girls.

To my parents, Tony and Linda Hamilton: Thank you for all of your support and sacrifice over the years. Our hard work paid off!

To my father-in-law and mother-in-law, Michael and Janice Chadwick: Thank you for never giving up on me and for loving me from day one.

To Jason, my brother: Growing up, you were a great brother, who never told me I was too small or couldn't accomplish anything. You are a good man, brother, and friend.

To my grandmother, Mary Holt: Thank you for the support over the years, especially when it seemed that everyone had given up on me, you took a chance. Thank you for telling me that I could when others had lost hope.

Roy Silver and Randy Holland at the Winning Inning,

Clearwater, FL: Without you guys, I would not be the man I am today. Thank you for all you have done for me.

Johnny Narron: Thank you so much for your support. It means the world to me. You are so much more than a mentor, you are a true friend. I treasure our friendship and I'm truly thankful for you.

Jerry Narron: Thank you for being a part of my first year in the big leagues. You were a great manager and friend.

Steve Reed and Ken Gamble: Thank you for helping and guiding my family through the difficult times and for sticking with us over the last ten years. You are both such special people and we are blessed to know you.

Pastor Jimmy Carroll: Thank you for your prayers and for being there to support and love my family. God has given you so much wisdom and I'm extremely grateful for your willingness to share it.

To the Texas Rangers: Thank you for allowing me to be part of the Texas Family and its wonderful fans. I am truly grateful for the opportunity to play for such a wonderful organization, which is so supportive of my recovery.

To Richard Abate, my literary agent: Thank you for all your hard work and tenacity in making sure this process ran smoothly.

To Harry Helm, my editor at Hachette Book Group: Thank you for believing in this project and having the vision to push it through.

Lastly, thank you to everyone who prayed for me. I do not take that for granted. It means more to me than you'll ever know. Prayer is one of the greatest gifts a person can give or receive.

There are sure to be more storms in life, but all of you have helped prepare me for them. Thank you so much! I love you all.

Beyond Belief

INTRODUCTION

IN LATE JANUARY of 2006, on the spongy green grass of a former spring training stadium in Clearwater, Florida, I stood on a baseball field with a bat in my hands for the first time since I could remember. Clean and sober for more than four months, I was stringing together so many good days I was starting to believe I would never have another bad one.

My wife, Katie, was in the stands to watch me take batting practice that day. She had never seen me play baseball before, and all she knew of me as a ballplayer was my résumé—number-one pick in the 1999 draft, minor-league MVP, consensus choice as the best prospect in baseball. But those accolades were in the distant past, clouded by the self-destructive path my life had taken over the past four years. Katie and I had been married for a little more than two years, and in those two years I hadn't swung a bat more than twice. She did not know me as a ballplayer. More than anything, my wife knew me as a flawed, sometimes-charming, sometimes-reckless drug addict.

But on this day she sat low in the stands on the third-base side of home plate to watch me take batting practice on the field with a group of seven or eight minor-league ballplayers whose agent had brought them to Jack Russell Stadium to get some work before spring training. I was the oddball of the group, the former phenom who hadn't played for nearly three years, the one-time legend whose repeated suspensions for drug use had already set a major-league record.

I bounced around the field like a child, laughing and joking and inhaling the smell of the fresh-cut grass deep into my lungs. This must be what it feels like to be released from prison. The other players looked upon me warily, not knowing how to square my tattoo-filled body and sordid past with the giddy man standing before them.

I had regained most of the fifty-five pounds I had surrendered to my crack habit, and I was trying to regain the life I lost along the way. As I prepared to hit, I looked at Katie and smiled. I was attempting to win her back, to reconcile our fractured relationship after so much disappointment and loss. I felt like I was in high school again, trying to impress a girl.

The wind blew directly into the batter's box from center field, strong enough to starch the flags in center field. The first few hitters drove low liners to the gaps and deep drives that were knocked down by the wind. To a man, they walked out of the cage muttering about the wind and complaining about how tough it was to hit under those conditions.

Katie was over there praying the whole time, worried that I was going to do poorly and somehow decide to give it up all over again. This was a pivotal moment, when I decided to put myself out there to salvage a career I had done everything to destroy. I could tell Katie was nervous, and I smiled from behind the batting cage and mouthed the words "Calm down, it's okay."

I hit last, and after a couple of swings I caught a groove. I was hitting balls all over the field, and more than a few over the fence. The guys milling around the cage stopped their conversations to lean on their bats and watch. This was what I used to live for—not the games or the money or anything else. I lived for the feeling I got when I stepped into the cage and everyone stopped what they were doing to watch and react. I lived to stand in that cage and pretend not to hear what they were saying when the ball rocketed off my bat and carried unimaginable distances. They whispered to each other, saying the same things I'd heard since high school. *The ball just sounds different off his bat. Did you see where that one went? This guy's amazing.*

It felt good to be back on a baseball field, and it felt good to be feeling good. I can't overstate the lightness it created in me to wake up with a clear conscience and go to bed the same way. Every day was progress, building my body up instead of tearing it down, and taking each day as a gift from God.

It seemed like this gift—this special gift to play this game—hadn't abandoned me after all.

When I finished hitting, the first thing Katie said was, "I felt sorry for those other guys."

"Why is that?" I asked.

"Because they're not very good."

"Sure they are," I said. "They're all professional players. Some of those guys will be in the big leagues someday."

"Well," she said, completely innocent. "Compared to you, they aren't very good."

I turned my head and looked at her out of the corner of my eye, as if to say, "What did you expect?"

That was the moment it dawned on her. All those things she'd heard about my ability on the baseball field, all those things pro scouts said about me when I was the number-one pick in the 1999 draft, all those things that made the Tampa Bay Devil Rays give me a record $3.96 million bonus out of Athens Drive High School in Raleigh—all those things were true. They were every bit as true as the nightmare she had lived with me, her drug-addict husband, ever since we got married.

Her jaw dropped open for a moment as the realization struck her. I could see her running it through her head—what she had just witnessed coupled with the torment of the past two years. She clenched her jaw and play-punched me in the shoulder. "I'm glad I didn't know this before now," she said. "If I had known you were throwing away *that* kind of talent, I would have been so much angrier with you."

CHAPTER

ONE

THE MAN WATCHED silently, his arms crossed. He sat directly behind home plate, halfway up the concrete bleachers, a lone figure in the West Raleigh Exchange ballpark. I didn't know who he was, or why he was there, but occasionally I'd catch my daddy glancing up at him from his spot on the field. They'd exchange polite nods like two men sharing a secret language.

I was practicing with my brother Jason's team, like I always did. The team, made up of eleven- and twelve-year-olds, was coached by our father, Tony Hamilton. I was six at the time, almost seven. I ran around shagging balls and getting to hit at the end of practice. Jason— whom I always called "Bro"—was always encouraging to me when he probably could have told me to stay home or at least stay out of the way.

The day the man sat in the stands, I made a diving catch in the outfield that nobody could believe. I was running from right-center toward center field and diving till my body was parallel to the ground as I caught a ball about six inches off the ground.

I was six years younger than most of the players on Jason's team, but I could do things on the field they couldn't do. I lived to play ball, and I had precocious ability from the time I picked up a ball. Bro and I would play in the yard or across the street at the cemetery, and I refused to accept our age difference as a valid reason for his superiority. I couldn't beat him—he's four years older than I am, and four years is a huge age difference for a long, long time—but I always thought I could. Whatever we played, whether it was basketball or wiffle ball, I went into every game convinced this was going to be the day.

The time I spent practicing with Jason's team was my favorite time of the week. My team, at the coach-pitch level, was not a challenge. When the season started, I was the typical little boy, thrilled to put on his baseball clothes and get to the season's first practice. Once I got there, though, I was disappointed that my teammates couldn't keep up.

My daddy coached my team, too, and my momma always came to our practices. After the second or third practice of my coach-pitch team, once we were in the car and nobody could hear, they told me they could tell I was easing up on my throws and maybe not swinging as hard as I could when I was taking batting practice.

"I don't want to hurt anybody," I told them.

They shook their heads. "You play the way you know how to play," Daddy said. "Those other boys need to get used to catching balls that are thrown hard, and if you start trying to hit the ball so it won't hurt anybody, you're going to get into bad habits that'll be hard to break. You need to be a leader and they'll catch up."

When I thought about it, I realized that Jason didn't let up on me when we were playing together, and he was four years older. These guys were my age, so maybe they would get better and learn to react the way I did.

The next practice I threw as hard as I could, and it resulted in some missed throws and some tears. I got up there and hit the way I would if I was playing in the cemetery with Bro, and my teammates kept moving back till there was nobody in the infield. The parents watching shook their heads and started talking and laughing among themselves. They'd never seen such a little person do the things I could do.

As we got closer to the start of the coach-pitch season, the parents started to wonder whether I could be moved up to a more advanced level. There was nothing malicious about their concern; a move would help everybody involved. They were equal parts amazed and afraid—amazed at the speed at which I could throw the ball and the power with which I could hit it, afraid that their less-advanced sons might find themselves unprepared and in the way of one of my throws or hits.

I could hear them up there, telling grandparents and friends, "That kid's going to hurt somebody." By the time I was six, I could throw the ball about 50 mph, probably twice as fast as most of the kids my age. The parents' concerns were legitimate, and they were never malicious or angry. In fact, they were very supportive of my quest to leave the team sponsored by Hamilton Machine—a business owned by my dad's cousin—and move up to play with my brother. The sooner the better, as far as they were concerned, since they believed it was just a matter of time before one of their boys lost a few teeth or got a concussion.

Their fears became real in our first game, when I fielded a ball at shortstop and threw it across the infield as hard as I could to get the runner. There was a problem, though—the first baseman either never saw the ball or didn't react fast enough to catch it. He stood there with his glove turned the wrong way as the ball smacked into his chest. He went down like a sniper got him, and I think he started crying before he hit the ground. I felt terrible.

■ ■ ■

The mystery man in the concrete bleachers stayed till the end of practice. Afterward, he came down and talked to my daddy. They walked off to where no one could hear them and spoke for a few minutes. There was some talk among the older kids in the dugout that he was there to see me, but I couldn't tell whether they were fooling with me.

When the discussion was over, my daddy and the man shook hands and the man walked to his car. We carried the equipment to the truck and waited. When Daddy climbed into the cab he looked straight ahead and said, "Well, Josh, that man I was talking to is the president of the whole Tar Heel League. He drove all the way from Charlotte to watch you play. He heard about you and needed to see for himself. And, well, you're on Jason's team now."

I guess you could say that was the first time I'd been scouted. I was six years old, closing in on seven, and Bro was eleven. In the Tar Heel League, his team was the equivalent of majors in Little League, and everyone on Bro's team was somewhere between fifth and seventh grade.

Until I showed up. When that happened, the team had acquired a first-grader.

I later learned the Tar Heel League had never done something like this before. The local board couldn't decide to do something that drastic, and the parents' complaints had traveled all the way to the top. The president decided he needed to see me before he made a ruling, and his decision made everyone in our pickup truck happy. I got to play on the same team with my Bro, and my daddy had to coach only one team.

I think it made everyone on my old Hamilton Machine team happy, too. They thought it was cool someone from their team got moved up, and they didn't have to worry about catching one in the teeth.

It wasn't all perfect, as my daddy found out soon enough. At our first game, after the lineup was posted in the dugout, I had a question.

"Daddy, why you battin' me last?" I asked in my six-year-old southern accent.

"'Cuz you're the youngest one, that's why."

I didn't like that answer, and every game I said something when I saw my name in the ninth spot in the order. "Come on, Daddy, what are you batting me last for?" He never budged, though. That nine spot always had the same name: J. Hamilton.

In my mind, the team's worst hitter hits last, and I wasn't the worst hitter on the team. I turned seven in May and two weeks later, I hit my first real home run. A twelve-year-old named Larry Trantham was pitching, and he threw me a fat one over the middle of the plate. The ball hit the bat square, right on the sweet spot of the barrel, and I drove it over the fence in left-center. It's hard to explain, but on contact, I felt nothing. It's one of the best feelings in the world.

■　■　■

Life in the Hamilton household revolved around family and baseball. You couldn't tell where one started and the other stopped—not on a dare.

I wasn't a bad student, but given the choice between playing ball and memorizing parts of speech, I wanted the ball.

It was a family tradition. My parents, Linda and Tony, met at a ballpark. My daddy was warming up for a softball game on one diamond while my momma was playing a game on a field next to him. He looked over once and saw her hit a ball about fifty feet beyond the left-field fence, and everyone on his team just shook their heads and pointed to the spot where the ball landed. The next time up, the same thing happened, except the ball went even farther.

At this point, my daddy had seen enough. He walked over to her field and told someone, "I've got to meet that girl." He did, and within weeks they were dating and before long they were married.

My father grew up on his family's hog and chicken farm in Oxford, North Carolina, about forty miles north of our house in a rural area west of Raleigh. Momma grew up in the house next door to us, on the same piece of property about fifty yards away from our front door.

Like everyone in this part of the world, we were surrounded by pine forests. To this day, I know I'm home more by the smell of those trees than anything else. Across the street there's an old, small cemetery where we used to run around and hit baseballs or golf balls, maybe shoot our BB guns. Five or six years ago someone was buried in an old family plot, but when I was growing up there wasn't much action there. Down the road a huge piece of land is owned by North Carolina State University, and our favorite fishing hole was on it, not more than a three-minute walk from the house.

We were never more than a mile from a good fishing hole.

It was a good childhood. We weren't rich, but I don't think we knew that. I don't think Jason and I knew what rich was. We played ball and went to school and pretty much had the run of the place. We hung out as a family and didn't see much need to go out, even as we reached high school age. We were pretty content in our little corner of the world. We had everything we needed.

My grandmother on my mother's side lived right next door to us, in the same house my momma grew up in. This was the place Bro and I went to be spoiled with cookies and ice cream and grilled-cheese sandwiches. Mary Holt is an old-fashioned southern lady, more of a friend than an authority figure. My nickname from the time I started playing baseball was "Hambone" and I called Granny "Grambone." If we got in trouble at home, we'd always find our way over to Granny's house to escape. Whatever we had done to get in trouble didn't seem like such a big deal to her. She was the safe haven, and it was a role she enjoyed. I think she had a soft spot for me because I was the youngest and I shared her name—Joshua Holt Hamilton.

Granny never missed a ballgame. We didn't make a conscious effort to invite her to the games; it was just understood that she would be ready to come with us when it was time to go. My games, Jason's games—it didn't matter. She was there. Before every game, for good luck, I would walk over to where Granny and my momma were sitting and give each of them a kiss on the cheek.

From the time we started playing baseball, one of the major lessons we learned in our family was to respect the game. And a big part of respecting the game was respecting the people you play with and against. My daddy went out of his way to make sure he wasn't favoring his sons on the baseball field, and since I always wanted to please him and my teammates, I usually packed up all the gear after practices and cleaned the dugout after games.

My ability drew more attention to me, but I always put pressure on myself to go beyond people's expectations. I didn't want to be treated differently because I was a good player; I loved to play the game, but it didn't mean anything beyond that.

My parents taught us to be humble. My mom was an awesome slow-pitch softball player, one of the best in the area. She played first base and pitched, and the tales of her hitting exploits are repeated to this day. People around Raleigh who watched her play swear she could hit a softball four hundred feet.

Our parents raised us on the idea that a ballfield was the best place to be. They believed that sports keep kids out of trouble and headed in the right direction, whether they pick up a ball after high school or not. My daddy loved sports and played baseball, but he grew up in a family that felt it was much more important to work on the farm than to do something frivolous like playing ball. The demands of work limited his opportunities to play sports, but he played whatever he could whenever he could—baseball, softball, football, martial arts.

My daddy is big and strong, country strong, with forearms like pillars and shoulders wide as a doorway. He never had any formal strength training, but he set the unofficial YMCA bench press record in Raleigh with a lift of 540 pounds.

His limited opportunity to play sports made him determined to make sure we were able to take advantage of every possible opportunity.

My daddy coached Jason and me until we got to high school, and he wasn't the type of dad/coach who let us do whatever we wanted. His teams were disciplined. He made us keep our shirts tucked in, and he preached accountability, making sure we never left our bats or any other equipment for someone else to pick up.

We rarely crossed him, but once when I was eleven I didn't run hard enough to first base on a popup and he got all over me. We were playing some kind of championship game, and he told me I embarrassed him on the field. He never stayed mad, but I knew better than to do it again. From then on, I ran out every ground ball and every popup like my hair was on fire.

I was never pressured to play ball. The perception of my parents as hard-driving stage parents was never accurate. I played because I loved to play, and because I was good at it. If I had told my parents that I didn't want to play baseball, I honestly think they would have been fine with that. They would have been surprised, but they would have thrown themselves into whatever activity I chose to replace it.

They made sacrifices for us. Jason and I knew it at the time, but I don't think we completely understood the level of sacrifice until we got older. Daddy was, and is, a hard worker who got up early in the morning to go to his job as a supervisor for the Wonder Bread factory in town. Momma worked for the North Carolina Department of Transportation. She washed our clothes after dark, when the utility rates were lowest, so we could save money to spend on gas and food for our baseball trips.

My daddy always made sure he had a flexible enough schedule to work around my baseball games. To do this, sometimes he had to go to work at some ungodly hour so he could get his work finished in time to leave for the game. I would hear him leaving the house at three or four in the morning during the summer after we had gotten home after midnight from an AAU baseball tournament somewhere in the state. His bosses, in general, were understanding and appreciated his devotion to both his job and his family.

He got a new boss when I was twelve, the summer after I finished playing in the Tar Heel League and started playing traveling AAU ball in the summer for a team in Raleigh. One Friday my daddy did what he always did when the schedule got tight: He got to work at 2:00 A.M. so he could leave by noon and drive me three hours to a game.

As he walked to the time clock to clock out for the day, this boss stopped him.

"Tony, where are you going?"

"Got a ballgame," my daddy said. "I'm done for the day."

"You know, I need you here this afternoon. You need to stick around."

My daddy explained the arrangement he had with the bosses at the factory. As long as he completed his work for the day and it didn't cause any disruption—and it wouldn't have in this case—then he was free to go. He was a dedicated worker and went out of his way not to cheat anybody.

The new boss wouldn't hear any of it. He repeated his desire to have my daddy stick around for the rest of the afternoon. At this point, my daddy felt he was being tested, challenged just to see how he would react. This was not always a smart move for the person doing the challenging. My daddy just stood there with his timecard in his hand, waiting for his boss to make the next move.

"Tony, I've got a question for you: What's more important, the ballgame or your job?"

My daddy didn't hesitate at all. He didn't answer him directly, but he looked this new boss right in the eye and slid his timecard into the clock until it clicked. He put the card back in the slot, calmly walked out of the factory and never worked another day for Wonder Bread.

■ ■ ■

We went to Rocky Mount, North Carolina, one year for an all-star tournament, and I pitched the first game. Early in the game I threw a pitch behind a little kid on the other team. When it was his turn to hit the next time through the batting order, he dragged his bat to the batter's box with tears running down his cheeks. He stood outside the box, crying and looking at the third-base coach to see if he might spare him this moment and send him back to the dugout.

Instead, the third-base coach walked toward him and said, "It's okay, get up there and hit. He's not going to hit you. Be a big boy."

He looked at the coach and sobbed, "It's too fast." By now everyone in the stands was trying not to laugh at this poor kid, who probably should have been allowed to walk back to the dugout and put his bat down rather than be scarred for life by his behavior in a Tar Heel League game.

Finally, he agreed to get in the box. Everyone cheered and told him he could do it. He stood as far from the plate as possible and looked ready to bail at any moment. He held his bat on his shoulder, showing no intention of even thinking of swinging.

And so I wound up, and threw.

I was eleven years old, and I threw the ball about seventy miles per hour. The problem was, I didn't always have any idea where it was going. Pinpoint control was not part of my game. I don't know whether hearing the coach promise that I wasn't going to hit him messed with my head, but I wound up and threw a fastball that thumped into the kid's back, right between his shoulder blades.

I felt terrible. This was the last thing I wanted to do, and maybe I tried so hard not to do it that I guaranteed that I would. I don't know, but if you thought he was crying before he got into the box, you can't imagine what he was doing now.

He was lying there perfectly still and screaming at the top of his lungs. "He hit me! He hit me!" It was like the ball stunned him or something, hit him right in the spine. The coaches and the umpire ran out to him, trying to convince him to get up and take his base, and he kept screaming: "I can't move! I can't move!" The only body part undamaged, it seemed, was his mouth.

In the course of all this screaming and crying, someone decided it would be a good idea to call an ambulance. I stayed on the mound, flipping the ball to myself repeatedly. It was a habit I had, part of my inability to be still, and also something I did when I was nervous or embarrassed. I didn't go down to the plate and get involved with the kid, though, because I was always taught to just throw the ball and not worry about hitting someone. I felt bad for him, but at the same time, it was his job to get out of the way of a bad pitch.

He stayed on the ground for what seemed like forever, long enough for the ambulance to arrive and the paramedics to get out to the batter's box. When they lifted up his shirt they saw the stitch marks from the baseball on his back. Eventually the paramedics and coaches convinced him that he could stand up and go on living, that he had indeed survived his encounter with this left-handed freak of nature and his wild fastball.

Years later, when I had been out of baseball and somewhat forgotten, my daddy was on a jobsite and he got to talking with some of the men there about baseball. He mentioned that he coached in West Raleigh, and this one guy said, "Do you remember that kid named Josh Hamilton who threw the ball a hundred miles an hour when he was eleven?"

My daddy said, "Yes, I do."

"Is that guy still around?"

"Yeah, he's still around. Somewhere."

"Well, one time I was playing against him and I didn't want to bat but they made me anyway, and he hit me right in the back. That hurt worse than anything in the world. I'll never forget that."

"Nope," my daddy said. "Neither will I."

"What do you mean? You were there?"

"Josh is my son."

The guy started laughing and shaking his head.

"You tell your son I never played past Little League after he hit me. That boy scared me to death."

■ ■ ■

There was a game in my last year in the Tar Heel League, when I was twelve years old, that I came to the plate five times and hit five home runs. I think after the third one the coaches and pitchers for the other team kept pitching to me just to see what would happen.

People saw me as different, something special, but they wanted me to succeed. I was always encouraged by other parents and coaches, and I attribute this to the way my parents taught us to behave. I never pimped a home run, not then or now, and I always went out of my way to praise my teammates for their achievements. I understood my talent for what it was—the ability to excel on the baseball field. It didn't deserve special treatment or a different set of rules.

During that summer, when I was twelve, I made my parents a promise. I said, "If I get drafted and get some money, I want you guys to retire. We'll use the money to pay off all your bills and you guys can come with me."

At twelve years old, I was good enough to dream. I could look around at the kids I was playing against and see that it wasn't a ridiculous leap to think that I could someday make money playing this game. My idea—to free my parents from all their hard work and repay them for their devotion—was a fantasy life as expressed by a twelve-year-old. Playing baseball for a living was the greatest thing I could ever imagine. My parents were always happiest when they were watching me play ball, so this seemed like the perfect solution for all three of us.

My parents tried to dismiss my comment.

"That sure is a nice thought, Josh," my momma said. "We'll see about that when the time comes."

I played basketball, too, and some soccer. When I was twelve, I played on a basketball team with Johnny Narron Jr., whose father was a major-league scout and a former minor-league ballplayer. Johnny Narron Sr.'s brother, Jerry, was a former big-league backup catcher who played eight seasons for the Yankees, Mariners, and Angels. At the time I started playing basketball with his nephew, Jerry was the third-base coach for the Texas Rangers.

The Narrons were a famous baseball family from Goldsboro, North Carolina, not far from Raleigh. Jerry and Johnny had an uncle named Sam who played in the major leagues for only twenty-four games—four in 1935 and ten each in 1942 and 1943. One of their cousins, also named Sam, pitched in one game for the Rangers in 2004. There were Narrons all over baseball.

The first time Johnny came to watch me play basketball with his son, he told someone in the stands he couldn't believe what a good athlete I was. As someone who was trained to evaluate athletic ability, his eye was drawn to me immediately.

"Those boys better be ready when he throws them a pass," Johnny said to some of the other parents. "I've never seen a twelve-year-old with that kind of strength."

One of the other dads told Johnny, "Well, if you think he's good at basketball, you ought to see him play baseball. He just plays this sport for fun. He plays baseball for *keeps*."

The parents proceeded to tell Johnny the stories about the Tar Heel League putting me on a majors team when I was six years old. They told him about my no-hitters on the mound and my four- and five-homer games at the plate. As a professional, he was used to hearing exaggerated stories from parents and friends, but these people had no reason to make bloated claims. He didn't let on that he was an associate scout for the Atlanta Braves at the time, but he filed it away and made a note to take the time to watch this Josh Hamilton kid play baseball before everybody knew who he was.

■ ■ ■

I played football my freshman year in high school, but after that my parents and I made the decision to concentrate on baseball. I was becoming strong, and the skills I picked up playing soccer (footwork) and running track (speed) would serve me well on the baseball field. My daddy started working with me on strength, buying a ten-pound medicine ball and giving me exercises to beef up my wrists and forearms to increase my bat speed.

Jason was out of the house by now, off at UNC Greensboro going to college and playing baseball. Jason was a power-hitting catcher who was a heck of a ballplayer—and a tough high school quarterback—but never quite good enough to be considered a pro prospect.

With Jason out of the house, my parents were free to direct all their attention toward me and my baseball career. I played varsity as a freshman at Athens Drive High School, and during that summer I started using a wood bat along with the standard aluminum high school bats. Without saying it, my daddy and I were pretty sure I was going to have the opportunity to play professional baseball directly following high school—that was the goal, anyway—and anything that helped me get there faster was worth the effort. And since professional scouts said their toughest job was projecting how well an amateur player could make the transition from metal to wood bats, we decided we would remove the mystery as best we could.

We thought of everything, or at least tried to. And if it sounds like pressure, it really wasn't. We were preparing for pro ball by the time I was fifteen, but the only pressure I felt was the pressure I put on myself. Baseball is a game of failure. You can't expect to succeed every time you go to the plate, or strike out every hitter, or throw out every baserunner. Accepting failure was the toughest lesson I had to learn. I was so hard on myself I had to fight the urge to expect perfection.

■ ■ ■

Johnny Narron returned to my life when I was fifteen years old. He asked me to play for a fall prospect team he was coaching. Johnny, who was still scouting for the Braves at the time, hand-picked the team based on ability. Johnny's son was on the team, and so was Matt Robertson, whose father, Jax, is an assistant general manager with the Pittsburgh Pirates.

Johnny couldn't wait for his brother Jerry to come home after the big-league season so he could watch me play. He told Jerry, "You've got to come see this kid; you're not going to believe him." I was playing anywhere—pitcher, first base, outfield, catcher, shortstop. I didn't care, as long as I was in the lineup and having fun. I loved to catch. Johnny would tell me, "You know, Josh, there aren't any left-handed catchers," and I would say, "I don't care, it's a lot of fun."

I don't know whether Jerry Narron got sick of hearing about this fifteen-year-old kid in Raleigh, but Johnny didn't get sick of telling him about me. The big-league season ended, and Johnny got right back to telling Jerry that he needed to come see me play.

"I'm coming out to see your son Johnny play," Jerry insisted.

"Oh, yeah, come see Johnny play," Big Johnny said. "But you've got to see this kid Josh Hamilton."

Johnny tells stories about what I did when I played on that team. Once we were running first-and-third plays in practice while I was catching and Matt Robertson was playing shortstop. I came up and threw the ball to Matt, who was cutting the ball off behind the mound, and it got on him so fast he either never saw it or couldn't react in time. It hit him right in the neck, and he went down like he might never get back up.

Another time I threw a ball from first to the short-stop to start a double play during infield practice and the ball tailed off just as it reached Johnny Narron. I threw it hard—probably too hard—and he couldn't stay with it. It caught him square in the ankle, and he walked with a limp for about a week.

This was a fifteen-year-old prospect team, and everybody on the team was identified as a potential star player in high school. I was part of the first wave of the specialized baseball teams—the travel teams, prospect teams, AAU teams—that are now a huge part of youth baseball. There weren't many rules; coaches or local scouts put together teams and then tried to find similar teams in the area to build a schedule. I probably could have been playing with the eighteen-year-old prospect team, but I was with my friends and besides, it was another example of people not wanting to set a precedent by advancing a player beyond his age group.

As Johnny Narron Sr., said, "A lot of times you see a twelve-year-old who is physically advanced, and eventually the other kids catch up to them. The strong kid matures earlier and is stronger, but he tops out. Things even out by the time he reaches high school. But in Josh's case, nobody ever caught up with him."

■　■　■

Ever since I was twelve, when I dreamed out loud about signing for enough money to pay off my parents' debts and bring them to the pros with me, I had my sights set on being a professional baseball player. I wanted to make sure

I took care of the details, and decisions such as hitting with a wood bat were calculated to maximize my chances.

This was a family thing. Everything I did was a family thing, baseball foremost among them. My daddy was part of the decisions I made, from using a wood bat to choosing the right summer team. But what some people perceived as pushing was simply supporting. The issue of hard-driving parents pushing their kids to earn a scholarship or get a contract is a serious one, but that wasn't what Tony and Linda Hamilton were all about.

Yes, we were preparing for the day when I could reach the level I wanted to reach. And yes, they were part of it. But they weren't stage parents, or helicopter parents, or whatever other negative descriptions you want to use. My parents never berated a coach or forced me to do anything I didn't want to do. I honestly think I could have decided to quit baseball and they would have been fine with it. They would have been disappointed, and they would have reminded me that I was wasting my God-given talent, but in the end they would have said, "Well, if that's what you want to do," and that would have been it.

That wasn't a factor, though, since my whole life revolved around the game. I developed routines the way big-leaguers did. I would park my '89 Camaro in the tree-lined parking lot behind the baseball field at Athens Drive and get dressed out of the trunk. I always blasted the same two songs: "Double Trouble" by Lynyrd Skynyrd and "Brand New Key" by Melanie. They were my baseball songs, and I never got sick of them. And I continued to kiss my momma and my granny before every game.

My daddy stopped coaching me before high school, and I brought the values he instilled in me to high school baseball. I always made sure to be respectful to the other team and the umpires. I always made sure to clean up the dugout after the game.

There were a lot of people who helped me improve, by giving me either instruction or opportunity. One of the men I always admired was Clay Council, who helped run the American Legion program in Cary. My brother played Cary Legion, and Coach Council was an assistant coach on that team. Whenever I didn't have practice or a game, I would go to Jason's practices and shag balls and hope to get in a few swings at the end of practice. That's how I met Clay—he would always have time to throw a few to the thirteen-year-old who was hanging around with his older brother. And he'd always smile and talk to me at the games when I was chasing down foul balls so I could get the free hot dog that came with every ball you returned to the concession stand.

Coach Council was a quiet, friendly man with a deep North Carolina drawl. He was about sixty years old when I met him, and he had already devoted a good part of his life to helping local teenagers become better ballplayers. He was a great batting-practice pitcher, and it seemed he could throw for hours and hours. As long as someone wanted to hit, Coach Council was there to throw.

He became part of the landscape of amateur baseball around Raleigh, and even though I played on the Fuquay-Varina Legion team, I would occasionally see Coach Council at the various high school fields, always throwing to whoever wanted to hit. Because my daddy was someone who volunteered his time to coach youth baseball, I was always aware of the sacrifices other coaches were making for me and my teammates. I noticed that ballplayers didn't always thank him for his time, and it made me more conscious of thanking him or any other coach.

Clay was one of those men who get forgotten when the boys pass through high school and move on to college or the pros. He worked at the Raleigh-Durham airport and spent much of his free time helping kids. He kind of blended in, never demanding anything, giving only instruction and encouragement. He and I both loved baseball more than anything in the world. I never felt as happy as I did when I was on the ballfield, and he looked like he felt the same way.

After I got drafted, I saw Clay at one of the fields during a Legion game and I told him right there, "If I ever get asked to be in the Home Run Derby, I'm going to ask you to throw to me."

I told him that every time I saw him after that, and he always had the same answer, "That's nice, Josh. I'd sure like that."

TWO

I NEVER HAD A PROBLEM with being the center of attention on the baseball field. It started when I was little, back when the president of the Tar Heel League showed up to watch me shag baseballs in the outfield of my brother's practice. I never sought out attention, but my ability brought it to me naturally. In a lot of ways, my parents and I had prepared for a time when the attention would turn from parents and teammates to scouts and college coaches, so when I entered my senior year at Athens Drive High, I had a pretty good idea of what to expect.

Or at least I thought I did, until it became a reality, and then I realized there was no way to prepare adequately for this amount of attention.

Baseball America magazine and every other publication that cared about amateur baseball rated me as one of the top five high school players in the country. I pitched, played the outfield, and sometimes played first base if I needed to either rest my arm after pitching or save it for an upcoming game. The only real issue for major-league teams was whether to draft me as a pitcher or an outfielder.

My preference was to be an outfielder, so I could play every day and do what I loved best—hit. But I had spent the time since the end of my junior year working out with rubber strength bands, and by the time my senior year started my fastball was clocked as fast as 97 mph. I understood it was a temptation for teams to consider using me as a pitcher, since left-handed power pitchers are the rarest and most valuable commodity in baseball.

By the time my senior season began, I had been told by more than one scout that I would be one of the top two picks regardless—pitcher or outfielder, it didn't really matter. In one of our early season games, with a line of scouts behind the plate, I was the starting pitcher and came out throwing bullets. The kids on the other team had no chance. My daddy was sitting close enough to see the readings on the scouts' radar guns—they were consistently 94 to 96—and after the second or third inning he walked down toward our dugout and got my attention.

"Josh, take a little off," he whispered.

I was confused. Nobody could touch me. I was blazing everybody.

"Why?"

"'Cuz if you keep throwing like that, all these scouts are going to want to make you a pitcher. Tone it down to about 90—they still won't be able to hit it."

If the scouts were unsure whether I was a pitcher or a position player, later in the game I gave them something that either further confused them or set their minds at ease. On one of the few decent pitches I saw, I hit a 450-foot homer into the football practice field beyond the fence in right-center. I was also walked intentionally three times, an event that happened way too often for my—and the scouts'—liking. They would grumble and groan about not getting a chance to see me swing the bat after they'd driven all day to watch me play. Some of the coaches we played against understood what was going on and actually allowed their pitchers to throw to me so the scouts could get a look. I hit over .600 my senior year, and I learned to become a pretty good bad-ball hitter because I was never sure I was going to get a decent pitch to hit.

On the days I pitched, I became accustomed to the choreography of the scouts as I stood on the mound and looked in for the catcher's sign. They stood—sometimes as many as sixty of them—behind the chain-link backstop and raised their radar guns to eye level in unison every time I started into my windup.

When I came to the plate, they all watched intently with their stopwatches in their hands, thumbs on the trigger, ready to click the second I made contact so they could time me running from home plate to first base.

Scouts are a traditionally skeptical bunch. Sometimes they fall in love with a player and exaggerate his abilities, but they're more likely to seek out flaws to hedge their bets. They rate players based on five tools—hitting for average, hitting for power, throwing, fielding, and speed. A player who is above average in three of those tools—or, in the scouting lexicon, "plus" in three tools—is considered a definite pro prospect.

Scouts throw around the phrase "five-tool player" the way they throw around concrete pillars. It's the most exclusive description in baseball, and from the time I was a sophomore in high school, it was the term most often used to describe me. Some of the quotations from the scouts in the newspapers were so flattering they bordered on embarrassing. They were comparing me to the great Mickey Mantle and saying I was the best high school baseball player they'd ever seen.

The scouts did their homework, too. They left nothing

to chance. When it became clear that I was going to be one of the top two players taken in the June draft, the intensity escalated. The Tampa Bay Devil Rays had the number-one pick, and the Florida Marlins had the second pick, and both teams made sure they knew all about me in advance of the draft.

They interviewed me, my teammates, my friends, my coaches, my parents, my brother, and pretty much anybody else they could think of. They would have interviewed my girlfriend if I had one. They put me through psychological testing to see how I would respond to tricky situations. They asked me unusual questions to judge my ability to think on my feet.

My senior year was like one continuous audition for the draft. My job was to impress these men who came to my games and came to my house to get to know me better. I already knew all the area scouts—the men whose job was to scout the Raleigh area for major-league teams—but my senior year brought out the cross-checkers and the player-personnel guys from the team offices.

When a team is looking at drafting a player high in the draft, they don't rely on the opinion of just one person. The investment involved dictates a variety of opinions, and national cross-checkers are the seasoned scouts who travel around the country assessing the players already recommended highly by the area scouts.

My status as a potential top pick increased the scrutiny exponentially. The teams drafting near the top sent not only area scouts and cross-checkers but scouting directors and even general managers. Even teams that realistically had no chance of drafting me, teams drafting after the fifth pick, sent cross-checkers to my games in case every team in front of them passed on me.

I talked to college coaches, also, and I made a verbal commitment to North Carolina State—about three miles from home—to make sure the pro scouts knew I understood the process and wasn't going to leave myself without leverage. But everyone, including me and my parents, knew college wasn't a legitimate option for someone who was being talked about as one of the top two picks in the country. Faced with the possibility of being given the job of my dreams after high school graduation, choosing professional baseball over college was an easy decision.

The talk of the draft created a buzz around the Athens Drive High campus, too. I'd walk out of a classroom and be met by several other students holding baseballs for me to sign. I always signed, even when it meant being late for my next class. Kids and even some adults crowded around after games to ask for my autograph, and I always took it as a compliment instead of an imposition.

At the beginning of finals week at the end of my senior year, I was faced with the daunting task of writing a final term paper for my senior English class. Reading and writing have never been my strong suit—an opinion shared by my English teacher. He offered me a deal: I could either write the paper or sign a dozen baseballs in exchange for an A in the class. That was an easy decision for me—I have to admit, I signed the baseballs—and I can tell that story now only because he no longer teaches.

With all this attention swirling around me, I knew I had to be smart about what I did and who I hung out with. I was a homebody, anyway, so it didn't take much effort for me to lay low in anticipation of the draft. I just didn't want to jeopardize what I'd worked so hard to achieve. I was a public figure, and my actions were being dissected from every possible angle. This was a strange situation for a seventeen-year-old, and I dealt with it by avoiding any situation that might turn out to be compromising. I didn't go to the prom my senior year because I didn't want to find myself in a guilt-by-association position. If someone around me was doing something wrong, I didn't want to be close enough to be implicated. In a funny way, it might seem that I had more sense and a stronger moral compass as a high school senior than I did later in my life.

My dream was so close to becoming reality, and I wanted nothing to get in the way. I had my eyes fixed straight ahead, on the draft and pro ball. After that, I would set my sights on making the quickest possible jump to the big leagues, where I could go about proving my daddy right when he told me, "Son, you're the best this game's ever seen."

■ ■ ■

There was a special-education student named Ashley Pittman who went to Athens Drive and worked as our bat boy/mascot. Ashley had Down syndrome, and he was one of the happiest people I've ever been around. He loved his job, and took it seriously. He dressed out in uniform for every game and came to most of the practices. I always enjoyed being around Ashley, and I considered him a friend.

One time Ashley came home with me for lunch and Granny cooked us some grilled-cheese sandwiches. This was a big deal to Ashley, and he was so appreciative you would have thought Granny bought him a new car.

We played in the state playoffs my senior year, advancing to the semifinals. We lost in that game, and afterward as we were riding home in the bus I noticed Ashley sitting by himself, crying.

I moved up to his row and sat next to him.

"What's up, Ashley?" I asked.

He didn't always understand why things happened on the baseball field, and for reasons known only to him he thought he was the reason we lost this game.

"I'm sorry, Josh," he said. "I'm sorry I lost the game."

This was ridiculous, of course. Ashley didn't hit or pitch one ball, but I couldn't put it that way for fear of hurting his feelings.

"Oh, no, Ashley," I said. "No one person ever loses a game for a team. We win as a team and lose as a team."

Immediately, Ashley's face brightened. He stopped crying and smiled at me as the tears streaked down his cheeks.

"Josh?"

"Yes, Ashley."

"Does that mean I'm part of the team?"

"Of course it does, Ashley. You know that."

His smile turned to laughter. He reached over and wrapped his arms around me, squeezing me tight with a big hug.

For the rest of the ride home, if you had looked at Ashley you would have sworn we just won the state championship.

At the banquet after the season, our coach got up and announced he was starting a special award to honor the Athens Drive Jaguar who best exemplified the qualities of compassion and sportsmanship.

When he finished the buildup, he said, "And the first winner of the Ashley Pittman Award is Josh Hamilton."

I always wanted to get along with everybody, regard–

less of who they were. In high school I could mingle freely with the jocks and the stoners and the kids like Ashley. I always tried to see the good in people, to live my life in the way I thought was best without judging people who took different paths. I don't know if my approach to life was Christian or naïve, but I didn't categorize people and automatically dismiss them. I wanted to be liked, and I thought it was a good thing to be able to find common ground with people with whom I had little or nothing in common.

I've gotten a lot of trophies over the years, but the Ashley Pittman Memorial Award is special to me. It's still prominently displayed in a case at my parents' house. More than any other trophy or newspaper clipping, it reminds me of who I was and how I lived at that point in my life.

■ ■ ■

Most of the top high school baseball players were dealing with college coaches, while I was dealing with agents and pro scouts. My parents and I had to choose an agent and a financial advisor before the draft, even though I couldn't sign with them or take any money until afterward.

Just as every player wants to be the top draft pick, every agent and financial guy wants to be able to say he represents the top draft pick. We had our choice of the best baseball agents and money people in the country, including the most famous agent of all, Scott Boras.

My parents set up the meetings with all the agents and financial guys. They came to the house armed with all their information, and I sat there bored. They were full of compliments and promises, and it was my parents' job to figure out who was honest and who was full of it.

This was a part of the process I could do without; I just wanted to play ball and let the rest of it take care of itself. My parents might not have college educations, but they were able to sniff out the phonies and the suckups. They narrowed the agent and advisor pool pretty quickly.

In the end, we chose Casey Close from IMG as the agent. Two guys from Northern California, Steve Reed and Ken Gamble, were the friendliest and most straight-forward money guys, and my parents hired them after they'd been in the house for less than an hour.

My daddy heard their sales pitch, then Ken and Steve spoke to me for a few minutes while my parents discussed it between themselves in the kitchen. When I was finished answering their questions, my daddy looked at Ken and Steve and said, "We've decided to go with you guys." They tried to contain their excitement, but it was clear they were pretty surprised to have been hired that quickly.

By this time, Boras was already known as the ultimate baseball super-agent. He had already caused some teams to recoil every time they saw a player represented by him, and that was one of the reasons we didn't choose him. From the beginning, my daddy told the agents and the teams that we weren't looking to fleece anybody.

"We don't want to take anybody to the cleaners," my daddy said whenever he was asked.

We knew the signing bonus for the first or second pick was going to be more than enough to last us for a long, long time. The most important thing was to get me signed for a fair amount of money and get me started as quickly as possible on my pro career. That was exactly what the Devil Rays wanted to hear.

About a week after the draft I received a letter from Boras. In it, he outlined the reasons why I should have signed with him. I didn't think much about it at the time, but it was probably a good business move for him to keep his name alive in my mind in case something didn't work out and I found myself shopping for a new agent.

As we got closer to the June 2 draft, the talk of the number-one pick narrowed to the two Joshes: me, and a hard-throwing right-handed high school pitcher from Houston named Josh Beckett. The Devil Rays would pick one Josh first, and the Marlins would follow by picking the other Josh.

About a week before the draft, it became clear I would be drafted as an outfielder. There was still some room for me to demand to pitch, if that was my choice, but I wanted to play every day and the two teams decided I was more valuable playing every day than I would be pitching every fifth day. As much as I enjoyed pitching, I agreed completely.

There hadn't been a high school position player taken with the number-one pick since Alex Rodriguez was drafted by the Seattle Mariners in 1993. The consensus among scouts who had seen us both was that I was a better high school player. Some of those scouts—again, people not naturally given to hyperbole—openly stated that I was the best high school player anybody had ever seen.

And three days before the draft, I got a call from Devil Rays' scout Mark McKnight. As the Devil Rays' area scout for North Carolina, he had become a fixture around my high school games. It's a once-in-a-lifetime experience for an area scout to be in position to recommend a player to be the top pick in the draft, and by the time the week of the draft arrived, McKnight probably knew more about me than I did.

After I came to the phone—with so many people

calling, I made it a point not to answer the phone during this stretch—McKnight said, "Josh, I'm calling to let you know we've made our decision. We're going to pick you number one in the draft."

This wasn't completely unexpected, but when he said the words all I could think to say was, "Wow." I thanked him and hung up, then told my parents the news. There wasn't a huge celebration, just some hugs and handshakes and congratulations. I didn't know how I would react if that dream came true, and when it did I wasn't prepared for how humbling it was. Of all the amateur players in the country, all the high school and junior college and college players, I was going to be the first player taken in the draft.

I kept lining all those players up in my head, endless rows of uniforms and equipment stretching to the horizon. And me, a kid from a corner of North Carolina, coming from a high school with no special tradition of baseball, a kid who learned the game from a father who never played baseball in high school, was about to have his name announced first on the morning of the 1999 baseball draft.

Being the guy picked "one-one"—first player, first round—meant I would be scrutinized even more, by a far greater number of people. More than any other player in the draft, I would be subject to the instant analysis of my performance. I would be either a great pick or a bust, and it wouldn't take long for the reviews to start coming in. I would carry a label with me forever, to the point where it seemed to affix itself to me like another first name: former number-one pick Josh Hamilton.

It was understood that being one-one came with a certain responsibility that extended far beyond draft day.

It was my responsibility to dictate whether the label would become a source of pride, or a burden.

■   ■   ■

The Devil Rays did their homework. They scrutinized Josh Beckett just as thoroughly as they did me. They watched him pitch and spoke to his friends. They analyzed and assessed until they could predict when he would take a deep breath and when he would stand on the mound and stretch his neck. It wasn't science, but they pretended it was.

My parents prepared for draft day—June 2—by planning a party at our house. People from the community, eager to get involved in an event that would attract the attention of the national media, offered their help. Pepsi donated drinks; a local pizza place donated food; a local funeral home provided big canvas canopies—normally used to cover gravesites at funerals—so everyone would have a place to escape the sun.

This was the beginning of my life's acceleration. Starting on this day, when the Devil Rays called my name in the morning, setting off a riot of cheers and laughter and hugs, my world became a blur.

I walked into the front yard and held my first press conference. The mood was happy and optimistic. When I was asked how I envisioned my career, I said, "I'm thinking three years in the minors, then fifteen years in the big leagues." I paused for a moment and said, "Then I'll have to wait five years to get into the Hall of Fame."

Everyone laughed, even the reporters. It was a moment when anything and everything seemed possible, maybe even probable. Nothing seemed too outlandish, not even crazy talk of the Hall of Fame before I'd even seen a pitch in the minors.

Still, crazy as it sounded, I was confident and eager to get started. I wouldn't have said those words if I didn't think they would come true. At that moment, with the world at my feet, that was exactly the way I believed my career would progress.

The festivities ended in the early afternoon. Nearly all the newspaper reporters packed up their tape recorders and notebooks and drove off. The television people got back into their vans and went back to the stations. We started cleaning up, and as we were breaking down the funeral-home tents, the one television reporter who lingered longer than the others asked us if we needed his help.

"Well, there is one thing," my daddy said, and I could tell right away he was about to launch into one of his practical jokes. "You see, the funeral home lent us these canopies to use for our party today, and when they delivered them I asked the director what we could do to pay him back. He thought for a minute and said, 'Bring me back some business.' And well, since you're the only one left here, I guess it's got to be you."

The reporter had been listening so intently to my daddy's story that it took a few seconds for him to realize my daddy was joking. Finally, he laughed and walked to his car with my daddy slapping him on the back the whole way.

When the yard was clear and the house empty, Jason and I jumped into the truck with our parents and went down to the high school to take some batting practice. Jason was home for leave from the Marines, and this seemed like the perfect way to celebrate the day. It was just like old times, the four of us doing what we loved to do.

There was a house beyond the center-field fence at the

high school, out in the pine woods. A family with two young sons lived there, and sometimes they'd come out and watch games or watch us hit. After I had been hitting for a few minutes, the young dad walked down to the field with his two sons. They watched for a while, and when I was finished he said to me, "I just saw you on the news, and I didn't expect you'd be out here tonight. But I can always tell when you're hitting. It just sounds different inside my house when your bat hits the ball. After the first crack of the bat today, my boys said, 'Josh is hitting.'"

In Houston, after being named the number-two pick in the country, Josh Beckett was given a Marlins cap to try on for the cameras. The cap was an adjustable-fit model, and as he worked to line up the holes to find the right fit, Beckett joked about the Marlins not being able to come up with a form-fit model.

In the *Raleigh News and Observer* the day after the draft, McKnight explained why the Devil Rays ended up picking me over Beckett. "I think character may have been the final determining factor," he said. "You read so many bad things about professional athletes these days, but I don't think you ever will about Josh."

At the time, he got no argument.

■ ■ ■

The day after the draft my parents and I flew to Tampa to be introduced by the team to the media and fans. On June 4, two days after the draft, I signed my contract in the morning. In the afternoon, I suited up in a big-league uniform—green jersey, white pants—with my name and No. 22 on the back.

I dressed in an unused locker in a corner of the clubhouse, and I tried to stay cool about the whole deal. Most of the other Devil Rays filtered past and shook my hand, welcoming me to the club and wishing me luck. I stood in front of the mirror in the bathroom and tried not to linger too long. I looked good, though, and I felt even better.

I took batting practice with the team, and they put me in the same group with Jose Canseco and Fred McGriff. Almost immediately, Canseco started calling me "Thumper," after the rabbit from Bambi. He saw my relatively skinny body— six-four and 190 pounds—and size-nineteen feet and decided I was the closest thing to "Thumper" in human form. After we'd taken a couple of rounds, he said, "Hey, Thumper, how about next round we have a home run derby, me and you?"

"Okay, sure," I said, figuring I couldn't say no and I really couldn't lose by saying yes.

He went first and hit three balls out. When he was finished, he leaned on his bat and said, "Okay, Thumper, show me what you got."

Surprisingly, I wasn't nervous. I thought it was funny, and I knew there was no way a kid two weeks past his eighteenth birthday could disrupt Jose Canseco's ego. So I smiled and nodded at Jose, respecting the distance of his shots, and proceeded to hit six homers in my next nine swings.

Six to three. Thumper wins.

Jose's three shots went a lot farther than mine. He hit two into the area they call The Beach above the second deck. But I was just eighteen years old, you know, and unlike Jose, I was working with God-given eighteen-year-old muscles.

When I walked out of the cage, I didn't say a word. And Canseco didn't say a word.

There was a weird quiet for a couple of seconds before I noticed McGriff. He was standing next to Canseco smiling while Jose ignored him. McGriff laughed to break the silence and said, "Challenge him to another one, Jose. Come on, challenge him again."

Canseco waved it off, like it was no big deal. I did the same, even though I was wishing I could tell everyone I knew what just happened.

Back in the clubhouse, as I changed out of the uniform and into my street clothes, Canseco approached me with a glossy folder in his hands. "Thumper, take a look at this," he said. I took the folder and saw a photograph of a beautiful Florida house, with all the pertinent information. It was a real-estate portfolio for a monstrous estate.

I looked at Canseco, a little bewildered.

"I'm selling my house," he said, completely serious. "You might want to take a look at it, see what you think."

I thought, Oh, man, this guy's something else.

In the span of three days, I'd gone from taking batting practice at Athens Drive High to being given the chance to buy Jose Canseco's house. None of this seemed real.

Before the game started I threw out the ceremonial first pitch. I stood on the front of the mound, while my mom, my daddy, and Jason stood to the first-base side of the mound. Jason was home on leave from the Marines, and as I wound up to throw I shot him a glance and winked before I tossed the ball to the plate. He started busting up.

All things considered, it was pretty crazy stuff for someone who was still two days away from high school graduation.

But in a weird way, I felt like I'd been preparing for this day all my life.

The contract negotiations didn't take long at all. Like

my daddy said, we weren't trying to squeeze the last nickel out of the Devil Rays. Casey Close, my agent at the time, handled the negotiations and everybody thought the outcome was fair for both sides.

In the meantime, I graduated high school and played two games for the local American Legion team. I hit three bombs in those two games, and my presence at those games attracted more attention. It was kind of a novelty act for the number-one pick in the nation to be playing in a local Legion game.

Everybody wanted to talk about money. "How much you getting?" "What are they going to pay you?" They looked at me a little differently because I was on the verge of a big payday. It made me a little uncomfortable; I was the same guy, doing the same things I always did.

In fact, I couldn't even answer when they asked about the money. I didn't have much of an idea about it. I wasn't involved in the negotiations, and I knew it was going to be enough to take care of me and my parents for a long time. That's all that mattered. I also knew I wasn't going to have more than twenty bucks in my pocket even after the contract was signed. My parents would see to that.

More than anything, I knew I was going to be able to make a living playing ball. Everything else paled in comparison to that one statement. That was all I needed.

The money bought freedom, the kind of freedom that allowed my parents to pull up stakes and go with me wherever the Devil Rays decided to send me. This was the fulfillment of the promise I made when I was twelve—I'd pay off my parents' debts and free them to travel with me.

My daddy took a leave of absence from his foreman's job at Ditch Witch, with the idea that he might never come back. My momma quit her job with the Department of

Transportation. We got word that I would be sent to the Devil Rays' Rookie League team in the Class A Appalachian League. We packed up and left for Princeton, West Virginia, the first step in the process of becoming a major-league star.

THREE

I GOT OFF to an inauspicious start. On the drive from Florida to West Virginia in the second week of June, we stopped at a gas station to fill the tank and get some food. I was starving, and I wasn't sure we were going to stop again, so I ordered a huge amount of gas-station fried chicken. This was my first big bonus splurge, I guess, and I ate like there was a hole in me somewhere. Within a couple of hours, I was sick as a dog, with vomiting and diarrhea like I'd never had before. My momma took one look at my green face as I walked out of a restroom at a gas station somewhere down the road and said, "Josh, you got food poisoning."

That was my first lesson as a professional athlete: Gas station fried chicken is a bad idea. I lost about eight pounds in three days and ended up in the hospital. The newspaper in Bluefield, West Virginia, had a big headline the next day: "Hamilton Hospitalized." If I thought I left the attention back in North Carolina, I was wrong.

The next day, my second day in Princeton, I saw the paper in the morning and noticed my picture on the front sports page. The story was about my expected debut that night, and the headline mentioned the "Record Signing Bonus" I received from the Devil Rays. I read the beginning of the story and that's when I found out how much money I had made—$3.96 million, a record for a number-one pick.

I sure didn't look like a multimillionaire. I walked into professional baseball wearing clothes bought at Sears and a gold necklace Granny gave me when I was in the tenth grade. My suitcase had a strip of masking tape on it with "J. Hamilton" written on it.

And my first home away from home turned out to be the Ramada Inn Limited in Princeton. The Devil Rays took up the first two floors of the motel, and my room was on the second floor, overlooking a family of skunks that lived in the field below. We bunked two to a room, and my roommate was a pitcher named Scott Vander Meer. He was probably the luckiest guy on the team; I was a great roommate because I was almost never there.

My parents rented a place close by, in a budget-suite type hotel. That had been the plan all along—since I was twelve years old—for my parents to accompany me to the minor leagues and for the three of us to live together when I got there.

Everything was new. Everyone on the team was either drafted or signed in June and sent to Princeton together to start our careers. Most of us were just out of high school, a few were out of college, and some of us were just out of the Dominican Republic.

The team had some of the brightest prospects in the organization playing alongside players they term "roster fillers" because every team needs to sign enough players to fill a roster. Some of the roster fillers wouldn't last the summer.

Our manager was Bobby Ramos, a former big-league catcher whose job was to be patient and firm at the same time.

We were paid $212 a week and given $20 a day for meal money on road trips. We traveled through Appalachia in an old, loud bus that sputtered and groaned like an infected lung. We had to wear polo shirts to the ballpark every day. We'd never been happier.

■   ■   ■

My clothes were always clean. Some of the guys didn't have a lot of extra clothes, and some of my teammates weren't fanatical about doing their laundry. My mom would take my clothes and make sure they were laundered and folded for the next time I needed them.

Some of my teammates tried to save money and eat one or maybe two meals a day. Some of the guys were sending a big part of their check home to the Dominican, and there were stories about some of my teammates' eating unbelievable amounts of food after being invited to eat dinner with some of the booster families. One newspaper reporter from the *St. Petersburg Times* followed me around for a series on my first weeks of pro ball, and she reported that one of my teammates ate twenty-seven pork chops one night at someone's house. That's got to be some kind of record, both for eating and for cooking.

Me? I always had plenty of food, and my bonus money made it easy for us to eat good food and not worry about setting aside the per diem to make ends meet. I was different. I was fortunate. My parents could afford to be there with me, and that worked to my advantage. I didn't have to worry about many of the things my teammates worried about. I could get to the ballpark early—I was always either the first one there, or very close behind the first one there—and I worked harder than anybody else. I wanted to be great, and I was willing to put in the work to get there.

My parents went to the ballpark every day when I did. They watched us work out on the field and take batting practice. They watched the grounds crew roll away the batting cage as it got closer to game time and line the field so everything looked sharp for the first pitch.

There were times when Ramos sensed we were dragging or that guys hadn't been eating properly. He would call one of my parents down to the screen behind home plate and ask them to head out to McDonald's and get thirty cheeseburgers or breakfast sandwiches for the team. He'd always try to hand my daddy some money through the screen, and my daddy always waved him away and went out to buy the food himself.

I can't count the number of times my parents got into the truck and drove one of my teammates who needed a ride back from the ballpark to the hotel, or someone who forgot something and needed to run back to the hotel to get it. In the Tar Heel League we always had team moms, and it seemed to me like my parents served as the team parents for the Princeton Devil Rays.

Even without Granny, I continued the tradition of kissing my momma on the cheek before every game for good luck. It was also a way of thanking her for being there. I saw no reason to change just because I was being paid to play. The place changed, but the particulars of my life didn't. In high school, my momma would get off work and come to the field to watch practice. And now, in Princeton, my parents came to the park early to watch batting practice and then waited for me in the parking lot after the game. From there, we'd get something to eat, usually at Applebee's, and talk about the game. I'd either head back with them and sleep in their suite or go back to the Ramada.

Most of the time — no, almost all of the time — I stayed with my parents. I didn't have any clue this would be seen as a bad thing, but after a few weeks I got the vibe that it was. The folks who ran the Devil Rays thought my parents' involvement was getting in the way of my becoming a man and learning to cope with life on my own. They also thought it was an obstacle to my bonding with my teammates.

One of my teammates, a pitcher named Charles Armstrong, was quoted in the *St. Petersburg Times* as saying, "This is the time to step into manhood. What are they doing here?"

I looked at it differently. They were here to make the transition easier, and we couldn't see how that could be seen as anything but positive. There was no doubt it was good for me; it was also good for the Devil Rays. They paid me nearly $4 million to play baseball and be as good as I could be. This was the best way for me to make their investment pay off.

We spent a lot of time in a corner booth at Applebee's. We'd talk about the game and go over each of my at bats. It gave me a lot of comfort to be able to do exactly what I did in high school, even though I was nowhere near home.

One of my Princeton teammates asked me how I handled having my parents around all the time. I told him I was fine with it, and he said, "Man, I couldn't stand having my parents around."

"That's you," I said.

Minor-league baseball can be a grind. You don't think about that when they're patting you on the back on draft day, but day after day, night after night, bus ride after bus ride—it wears on you. We'd get our twenty-dollar-a-day meal money on the road and eat at Wendy's or McDonald's or Po' Folks. We'd play three games in one small town in the Appalachian League—Johnson City, Tennessee, or Bluefield, Kentucky, or Pulaski, Virginia—and then move on to the next. We'd wake up and have to check a schedule to see where we were.

Some guys couldn't hack it and got cut. Some guys couldn't hack it and just left. They'd say good-bye to the skipper and head for home. They gave it their shot and made up their mind. A lot of guys got to pro ball and discovered their limitations. They saw how good other guys were and had to assess their own abilities.

If you came to the conclusion this was the highest level you could hope to reach, that your career would never advance past the dingy motel rooms and smelly bus rides, it wasn't a hard call. Sometimes we'd go out to play on a Sunday afternoon and there'd be fewer than fifty people in the stands. For the first time in any of our lives, baseball could feel like a job.

There were several Dominican players in Princeton, as there are at every level of baseball, and for the most part we all went our separate ways. Baseball is kind of that way, mostly because of the language barrier. I got frustrated because I couldn't communicate with these guys—I knew no Spanish and they knew very little English. I talked to a high school Spanish teacher and had her teach me how to say some simple Spanish phrases. I wanted to be able to tell my teammates good game, or maybe be able to call off the second baseman to avoid a collision on a popup.

My parents and I talked about the language difficulties, and how fortunate I was to be able to spend all this time with my parents while easing my way into pro ball.

My daddy would say, "Put yourself in their shoes, with no one around to look after you so far from home." Many were homesick, and I know they would have loved to have had their parents around.

Carl Crawford was a second-round pick from Houston, a bundle of raw talent who ran so fast your eyes had to work to keep up with him. He signed for $1.5 million, also out of high school, so between the two of us we accounted for almost $5.5 million worth of bonus money the Devil Rays paid out in the draft. They expected to see a lot of the two of us, as well as top prospect Rocco Baldelli, in the outfield at The Trop for many years to come.

Despite our different backgrounds, Carl and I became friends and hung out some on the bus trips. Carl was good for my ego. Now a regular All-Star in the American League with the Rays, he is a fun, demonstrative guy who doesn't hold much inside. I'd make a play in the outfield or hit a booming home run and he'd say, "Hammy, you're the best I've ever seen." Sometimes it was simpler: "Boy, you can flat play."

From the first week we played together in Princeton, we talked about playing together in the big leagues. "Imagine how much ground we could cover in the outfield," Carl would say.

Carl had amazing energy, especially as an eighteen-year-old loving life in the minor leagues. He could get the whole bus rolling in laughter talking about his neighborhood back in Houston's Fifth Ward. I loved listening to Carl go on and on. Baseball had taken me out of my cocoon in Raleigh, but this was something different. I was spending most of my time with guys from the Dominican Republic, Puerto Rico, and Houston's Fifth Ward.

Carl kept his eyes open for the ladies. He'd look around

the stands before a game, assessing the situation, then he'd let us know what kind of night it was going to be. Once, in a scene recounted in the *St. Petersburg Times*, he assessed the crowd in Princeton and said, "So many goddamned women." And then he said, "All the girls do anyway is ask, 'Where's Josh?'"

During a food stop on one of our bus rides, he and I shared a table at Wendy's. We were wolfing down fries and burgers, and I was looking at the tattoo he had on one of his arms. It was a Rottweiler's face, and I told Carl I had been thinking about getting a tattoo myself. It was the first time I had told anyone that, but I had been looking at the tattoos of some of the other guys on the team and it seemed like a cool thing to do.

"Well, get yourself one," Carl said. "I know you've got the money."

"Nah, my parents wouldn't like that," I said.

Carl looked at me. It was like we came from different planets. He didn't understand why my parents would have anything to do with it.

"You can do what you want," he said. "You're an adult."

I gave him a look that made it clear I wasn't too sure about that. We laughed and changed the subject. I was an adult? I don't think I'd ever thought of it that way before.

■ ■ ■

The scene: a night game at Hunnicutt Field in Princeton, West Virginia, during my first summer as a professional ballplayer. A thunderstorm was moving in from the west, and I was playing center field in the late innings. Typical of ballparks in the low minors, the stadium lights were adequate but nothing like the big leagues, where it can seem like midday at midnight. Our manager walked to the mound to make a pitching change, and as our new pitcher was warming up I watched the clouds moving toward me.

There was lightning in the distance, and the clouds lit up every few seconds as they bounced our way. I watched, interested in the formations and curious about whether they would arrive and wash out the game.

I have difficulty describing what happened next. The clouds kept moving, and suddenly a demon's face appeared, superimposed on the clouds. It was jumping out at me, and it made me rock back on my heels. I got chills. The face was grinning, almost taunting.

The vision stuck with me the rest of the game. I didn't know what to make of it, but I didn't feel I could ignore it. There was something there for me, some message or warning.

After the game, I told my parents I was tired and wanted to head back to the room and get some sleep. My room-mate Scott and I walked back to the Ramada together. It was a quiet walk, but as we got within range of our room, I could see a blue flicker bouncing on the curtains. A light was on in the room, also.

"Didn't we turn the television off?" I asked Scott.

"Yeah, we did. And the lights."

"That's kind of strange."

Scott shrugged, obviously not giving it much thought. I unlocked the door and walked in. After what happened at the game, I was on guard. Scott walked straight to the bathroom, obviously figuring we just forgot to turn everything off when we left for the ballpark. To him, it was no big deal.

I looked at the television and stopped cold. A buzz ran

right up my back to the base of my skull. On the television I saw a white-and-gray cloud formation, similar to what I saw in the evening sky. Inside those clouds I saw a profile of what I believed was Jesus, reaching out his arms to me. He was superimposed on the television screen the same way the demon thrust himself through the clouds.

Obviously, these events were connected. There was a message being sent. It was my job to figure out what it was.

I went to bed that night thinking about my relationship with Jesus. I believed in God, but our family was not especially religious. We believed in God and treated others with respect and dignity. But I was clearly being asked to do more. I was being shown signs, and I needed to answer with a more devoted commitment.

So, with the events of that night providing the push, I lay in bed in a West Virginia motel room and thought seriously about the role of Jesus Christ in my life, and how I was supposed to respond to His message.

■ ■ ■

Vince Naimoli, the owner of the Devil Rays, flew into Princeton on August 16 to watch us play before the season ended. This seemed kind of different—why would he want to be in West Virginia in August?—but what did we know? We were first-year ballplayers just out of high school or college or just off the island. We weren't exactly experts on the behavior of big-league owners.

By the time we got to the park, word had circulated that Naimoli was there to watch me play. I had lived up to the lofty expectations so far, hitting well over .300 with power. That night, with less than two weeks left in

Princeton's season, I hit for the cycle for the first time as a professional.

After the game, I was called into Ramos's office.

"Congratulations, Josh," he said. "You're going to Hudson Valley in the morning."

I really didn't believe it. I certainly didn't expect it. I figured I would at least finish out the year in Princeton and then either move up or go home. I was hitting .344, so a promotion wasn't completely out of the question, but the timing was unusual. Apparently the purpose of Naimoli's visit was to take a look at me and make the decision on elevating me to the next level.

After he assured me he was serious, Ramos reached under his desk and pulled out a box of brand-new Appalachian League baseballs. He pushed them across the desk and asked me to sign them.

I was three months into this new life, and I didn't think it was strange that a grown man—a former big-league ballplayer—was asking me to sign baseballs for him. I had signed autographs in high school, but the onslaught of attention after I was the number-one pick was crazy.

Stuff with my name on it got stolen all the time. People sent me cards from all over the country. Some of them were baseball cards printed after the draft, but other people just sent blank stuff—index cards or pieces of paper—for me to sign and send back. My momma took care of all that, and she decided I wouldn't sign anything except baseball cards. If I signed a blank card or piece of paper, how would I know where it might end up? Someone might use it in the wrong way, or to suggest I was endorsing something I wasn't. I didn't want to have to think about all this stuff, and I realized right away that some of this stuff was never going to make sense.

But I sat there and signed all twelve baseballs for Bobby Ramos. When I was finished, I shook his hand, thanked him for all he'd done for me, and walked out the door, into the next phase of my life.

■ ■ ■

The Hudson Valley Renegades were in the late stages of a pennant race when I showed up the next day. The New York–Penn League was also short-season A ball, but the level of play was much higher than Rookie League. Most of the guys were older, many of them drafted out of college and some of them in their second or third year of pro ball. I had been playing with boys, but as I looked around the clubhouse before my first game, I saw a room full of men.

Hudson Valley was where I found out definitively that the Devil Rays had some issues with my parents' following me through the minors. Before they told me I had been promoted, they set me up with a host family in Hudson Valley. Instead of renting out floors in a motel, as was the norm in rookie ball, New York–Penn League teams housed their players with booster families. The Stewarts were retired schoolteachers who lived in Poughkeepsie in a two-story house with a hot tub. They already had two players from the Renegades living at their house, outfielder Matt Diaz and pitcher Derek Anderson.

The Devil Rays called them before I arrived to see if they could find room for another player for the remainder of the season. They agreed, and when the team announced the promotion they told me about my new living arrangement.

My parents didn't seem to have a negative impact on my play on the field—I hit .347 with 10 homers and 48 RBIs in those 56 games. I did everything the coaches

asked of me, but there were grumblings in the organization about whether my parents were suffocating me. Some
people felt I needed to grow, and my parents were seen as
an obstacle to that growth.

This is what got lost in the concern over my parents:
They never meddled. They didn't do anything but support me, whether that meant cooking for me or hanging
out with me or making sure I had everything I needed.
I was eighteen, just weeks past high school graduation,
and I wasn't ready to go out on my own. Every person
in the stands and every person in the towns we visited
knew I was "The $4 Million Man." My teammates rou-
tinely joked with me about the size of my signing bonus.
It wasn't mean, and it wasn't anything I couldn't handle,
but it showed how people looked at me now.

Weeks earlier I was a high school kid hanging out at
practice with my friends. Now I had a job, and all this
money hanging over my head. With all that going on, it
felt good to look up into the stands and see two familiar
faces. I didn't want to think about jumping into this world
with a bunch of money in my pocket and no experience,
managing a complicated life. It seemed like a stupid idea.

My parents attended every game, but they sat high
up in the stands, away from the scouts and the coaches.
They continued to arrive every afternoon or morning for
batting practice, and they continued to mind their own
business.

They were just there, supporting me and making sure
I wasn't overwhelmed by the experience of being the
number-one pick and starting my professional career. It
was all happening exactly the way I wanted it.

The team, however, thought it was a better idea for me
to live with strangers.

Everyone on the Hudson Valley team lived with a host family, so maybe the Devil Rays didn't want to set a precedent or give the impression that I had my own set of rules. Usually the families are members of the teams' booster clubs, and they house two or three players for the summer.

This was a very strange experience for me; my parents were living in a motel nearby and traveling to all the away games, and I was living with these people I had never met. It almost felt like being adopted by strangers, with my parents watching. Very strange.

They were an older couple whose children were grown, and they looked forward to the baseball season every year. The host-family program was a cool thing for them. My room was a foldout couch in the basement. I have to admit, I didn't spend much time there. I was in Hudson Valley for sixteen games, and half the time we were on the road. I probably slept at the Stewarts' house at most eight times. The other nights I stayed with my parents.

There was another reason I didn't understand the fuss about my parents: I didn't spend that much time with them, either. On a typical day, I would get to the ballpark around noon, work out in the afternoon, and play a game at night. I'd get back to the host family's house around 11:00 P.M. and then start all over the next day. There wasn't much time for anything but baseball and sleep.

My parents traveled with us on the road, though, and stayed in the team hotel. My time away from the ballpark on the road was spent with them. We would eat breakfast and lunch together, and they would obviously attend every game, and we might grab a bite to eat afterward. I was nineteen years old, and this felt perfectly normal to me.

Hudson Valley was a fun stop. I was dropped into the middle of a tight pennant race, and after a slow start with the bat I became a major contributor to a team that eventually won the New York–Penn League championship. The season ended with us dogpiling near the mound, happy as can be. If you ignored the small stadium and the uniforms and the peach-fuzzed faces of the ballplayers in question, you could have fooled yourself into believing we had just won the World Series.

However, the living arrangement issue created some friction. Years later, the Stewarts were interviewed by Dave Sheinin of the *Washington Post*, and Al Stewart said of my parents, "We disagreed with how they went about it, but it wasn't our place to say anything. We both thought one of these days he was going to break out. We didn't think it was going to be anything like this, but we knew there was going to be a backlash."

I guess everyone is an expert after the fact. However, I find it funny that people who knew me for maybe two weeks—tops—could make such sweeping proclamations about me, my parents, and my character.

Spending time with my teammates away from the ballpark was never a priority for me. My parents discouraged me from going out with teammates after games, mostly because most of the postgame activities—drinking, hanging out at bars, staying up too late—were not positive. It's a fact that baseball players do things after games that aren't productive. For years managers have been saying nothing good happens after midnight. I was serious about my job, and my job was to be ready to play every day to the best of my abilities.

I didn't know why I should be judged by what I did away from the field. I had great relationships with teammates at the ballpark, and I was never accused of setting myself above my teammates. They had their lives, I had mine.

Why was it better for me to live with strangers rather than my parents? I never got a satisfactory answer to that question.

■ ■ ■

In the spring of 2000, I was invited to big-league camp for spring training. This was more of a courtesy than anything else, a chance for the Devil Rays to see their number-one pick from the year before compete and associate with big-league ballplayers. Obviously, after one year in the low minors, I had no delusions of grandeur. I knew I was ticketed for another year in the low minors.

And so it was no surprise that I was assigned to the Class A Charleston RiverDogs of the South Atlantic League. The Sally League, as it's called, is a higher level than the short-season leagues I had played in during my first year, and many of the players had been in pro ball for three or four years.

My parents and I went to Charleston to look for a place to live—we were on our own this time—and we met a man named Richard Davis. He was a Charleston guy who loved baseball and helped us find a condominium to rent. Richard became a good friend of ours, and we spent a lot of time with him in Charleston.

My parents' routine didn't change. They continued to arrive at the ballpark early to watch batting practice. They traveled to all the road games and stayed in the team hotel in each city. To them, it was like being a fan of a team and having the means and the opportunity to follow it around for an entire season. Again, to me, it was no big deal.

I don't want this to be misconstrued as bragging, but I have always loved to listen and watch people's reaction when I'm taking batting practice. With the RiverDogs, my teammates looked forward to watching me hit every day. The opposing team would look up from their stretching to see how far I hit the ball. The fans in Charleston and the other South Atlantic League towns got to the park early so they could watch.

It was the first time I became aware of being good for business.

The best feeling in the world is to be standing in the batting cage hitting bombs and hearing people oohing and aahing as they watch the flight of the ball. It's even better when it's coming from players — guys who are pretty good themselves and not always free and easy with the compliments. I came to believe the four greatest words in the English language were "Did you see *that*?"

I was selected to play in the Futures All-Star Game, which was held July 9, the day before the major league All-Star Game at Turner Field in Atlanta. I played right field for the United States team against the World team. I went 3 for 4 in that game and we won, 3–2.

The game served as an exhibition, a chance for baseball to showcase its best young talent and get some of our names and faces into the minds of the fans. The big news — if there was big news to come out of a minor-league all-star game — came during batting practice, when Beckett and I met for the first time while standing in the outfield shagging baseballs.

The two Joshes, subject of so much speculation before the 1999 draft, were right where everyone expected them to be — on the fast track to the big leagues. We spoke briefly in the outfield, and he lent me his sunglasses when

I realized how much trouble I was going to have with the late-afternoon sun in right field. I had forgotten mine.

In all, my second season in pro ball went according to the script I had written in my head. I hit .302 with 13 homers and 61 RBIs, and after the season I was named the South Atlantic League Most Valuable Player. I was named the Player of the Year in Class A baseball, and the Devil Rays awarded me the Minor League Player of the Year for the organization.

Everything was falling into place. I started to think about accelerating my stated three-year timetable and making a run at a major-league roster spot for the 2001 season. The Devil Rays' big-league team completed another last-place finish, and the team seemed intent on going with younger players after a few failed seasons with a roster of veterans. The Jose Canseco–Greg Vaughn era didn't work, so I was hoping they'd try out a Hamilton-Crawford era.

I was getting stronger, becoming more of a man and less of a boy, and I vowed to use the off-season to increase my strength.

When they announced I had been given the league MVP award, my daddy shook my hand and said, "You're on your way, Josh." He was proud and I was happy, but there was a sense of inevitability about the path my career had taken.

After all, this was the way we expected it to be—certain milestones needed to be met on the way to the ultimate destination. A Class A MVP award was nice, but I had to believe there was more out there where that came from.

CHAPTER

FOUR

IN THE WINTER months after the 2000 season, with an MVP to my name and thoughts of the big leagues bouncing through my head, I spent a good part of the off-season in the Tampa area, in a small house we bought to use during spring training and, with any luck, the regular season.

My parents stayed home in Garner, outside Raleigh, in the big ranch house on twenty-two acres we bought to be our family's main home. While I was working out and getting ready for the season, I made a decision: I would get a tattoo. A growing number of players had them, and since that day in Wendy's with Carl Crawford I had secretly — at least secretly as far as my family was concerned — wanted to get one. I found a tattoo shop, and walked in and asked for my nickname — Hambone — to be tattooed in all caps around my right biceps.

I didn't announce the tattoo's arrival to my parents, but the next time I was home I showed it to my momma, and she was predictably upset.

"God gave you a beautiful body," she told me. "Why are you ruining it?"

"I don't know, Momma," I said. When I saw how much it bothered her, I said, "I promise I won't get no more."

The promise was halfhearted. To me, a tattoo wasn't an act of rebellion. I'm sure there was some declaration of independence included in the decision to do this, knowing they wouldn't approve, but I wasn't actively attempting to make anyone angry. I just wanted a tattoo, that's all. They didn't understand that. And over the next few months, leading to spring training, I decided I wanted five more.

■ ■ ■

So. The path to self-destruction—where did it start? Did it start with an automobile accident? Loneliness? Boredom? Weakness? Could it have been something as superficial as those six tattoos? It's easy to say my first taste of independence led me down a path to self-destruction, but I'd argue it was a little more involved than that.

When I walked into the clubhouse for the first time that spring, in mid-February 2001, those six tattoos, all on my upper arms and chest, created quite a stir. Judging by the reaction, you would have thought I walked in carrying an Uzi and telling everyone to hit the deck.

I changed out of my street clothes and into my uniform and, one by one, the players who knew me did a double-take. They'd look, then realize what they'd seen, then jerk their heads back and look again in disbelief.

First baseman Steve Cox walked over to me as I stood at my locker and asked, with mock seriousness, "Josh, is that you?"

I had two tattoos on each arm and two on my chest. The ink became the talk of camp for a few days. Guys I had played with in the minors knew me as the All-American Boy, the guy who kissed his momma before every game and did everything the right way. I was the straight arrow, the guy the Devil Rays drafted number one partly because I had shown no inclination to color outside the lines.

Now they looked at me and their eyebrows nearly arched to the ceiling. I didn't act differently. If I had kept my shirt on, nobody would have noticed.

The next day in the *St. Petersburg Times*, Marc Topkin wrote:

> Hamilton showed up early for spring training saying the attention and accolades of being one of the game's top prospects hadn't changed him, that he was still the same shy and humble kid from North Carolina who lived with his parents.
>
> And then he took off his shirt.
> One, two, three, four, five, six tattoos now adorn his upper body: a nickname and a symbol on each arm, and a pair of designs on his chest. You only had to watch and listen to the reaction of the other players to understand what a shocking development this was.

There was HAMMER on one arm and HAMBONE on the other. There were tribal designs on my chest. There was a part of me that enjoyed surprising them, in much the same way I enjoy hitting a ball in batting practice that has everyone buzzing and trying to figure out how far it went.

This story went beyond the tattoos and into the issue of my parents' influence on my career. Since it was unusual for a minor-leaguer's parents to travel with him and live with him, I understood the interest but wondered if the team wasn't going out of its way to look for something negative after an overwhelmingly positive start to my pro career. And given the "shock" generated by my tattoos, it was natural to ask my parents what they thought of the "new" Josh.

"It's just him trying to say, 'This is me,'" my momma told Topkin. "If this was rebellion, he'd be out drinking and partying and whatever the other guys are doing. So far, knock on wood, we don't have anything to do with that."

And my daddy said, "Put it this way: If this is the worst thing he ever does, I'll be happy."

■ ■ ■

The tattoos represent one notch on the timeline of my life. Some people, my parents included, would call them red flags. There is another event, a car accident, and this one grows in importance with each telling. It is a convenient starting point, serving as a ready-made catalyst for everything bad that happened afterward.

So, since it's kind of a habit, let's start with the events of March 3, 2001.

We had just started spring training games, and I got to the ballpark in the morning in preparation for the game that afternoon. I was having a good spring training, and there was some discussion circulating around the team that I might have a chance to break camp with the big club and start the season in right field.

I got called into manager Larry Rothschild's office. He waved me into a chair on the other side of his desk and shut the door. I had absolutely no idea why I was there.

This was my second spring training with the big-leaguers. The year before, it was more of a courtesy, a nod to my status as the number-one pick. It gave the folks running the team a chance to see me interact and play on the same field with the older guys. This time, though, there was a new feel to it.

It was the feeling that comes with expectations.

Rothschild took his seat and leaned back.

"Josh, if it were up to me, you'd start the season with us," he said. "But it's not up to me, and the decision's been made that you're going to start the season in the minors."

I was disappointed but not completely surprised. I hadn't played above Class A and knew it was a long shot, but I thought I'd get a chance to play at least two weeks of spring games before a decision was made. This removed the suspense pretty early in the process. From that standpoint, I left the manager's office a little deflated.

It made me wonder if the behind-the-scenes concern over my parents' presence in my life was an excuse to keep me in the minors for another year. The fans were clamoring for change, and if the Devil Rays didn't think I was ready to step into the big-man's world of the major leagues, they could point to my parents as an indication of why I wasn't quite ready.

After the game, I got into the truck with my parents and told them what Rothschild said. "Guess I won't be in the big leagues this year," I said. My daddy reminded me that I always said three years in the minors, and this would have put me a year ahead of schedule. Not many guys make the big leagues at nineteen, he said, so keep your head up, have a good season, and you never know what might happen.

We talked about that day's game, as always, and I told them I was going to be starting the next day against the great Greg Maddux. I'd heard so much about Maddux that I was excited about facing him; it was like stepping into baseball history.

We were driving through Tampa to our house near

Bradenton down one of those endless four-lane roads that connect Tampa with the outlying cities. My mom was driving our Chevy Silverado Southern Comfort edition, I was in the passenger seat, and my daddy was in the seat behind me. We were the third car in line, and as we drove through the intersection of Victory Road and Interstate 301, a yellow dump truck ran the red light and headed right for the driver's side of our truck.

It was like a slow-motion moment, where I could see it coming but felt helpless to do anything about it. The truck was heading right for my mom, and I reacted by reaching over and grabbing her by the shoulders. I pulled her toward me, away from the door and the point of impact.

Our truck jumped when the dump truck hit the left front of the truck. We started spinning and didn't stop till we'd gone about a hundred feet from where we started. My mom couldn't move. My daddy smashed his head against the window behind me. I felt something tweak in my back. Someone called 911 and the firefighters had to extract my mom from behind the wheel. They weren't sure she would have made it if she had stayed close to the door.

My mom had had neck surgery six months before, and a jarring automobile accident definitely wasn't in the doctor's post-op orders. She and my dad were taken to Memorial Hospital, where an X-ray showed my dad had a skull fracture. My mom's neck was sore, probably nothing more serious than whiplash. I was luckiest; they couldn't find anything wrong with me. All in all, considering what could have happened when we got hit by a dump truck traveling at about 40 mph, it seemed like we got lucky. We took inventory of ourselves and thanked God for our good fortune. It shook us up, but it certainly didn't feel like a watershed moment in my life.

Shortly after the accident, my parents left me in Tampa and returned to our house in Garner. I stayed by myself in the house we had recently bought near Bradenton. This is where you should hear the ominous music in the background, portending disaster. Alone for the first time, the sheltered young man faces an uncertain future. Those are the ingredients. When mixed, do they create disaster?

Most people thought my parents went back to North Carolina because of the accident, but they were planning on leaving all along. The accident had nothing to do with it. My mom had to go back to be near her doctors to continue treatment for her neck. I knew they were leaving before the dump truck entered our lives.

I might joke about the importance ascribed to this time, but I won't downplay the importance of finding myself alone for the first time in my life. I've always struggled with free time. I like to keep busy, keep moving. I need to be doing something, and I like being around people. It's the ADHD in me.

And after the accident, my back didn't feel right. I had pain in my lower back that felt like a knife jabbing at me. In workouts and on the field, it kept me from going full speed. These events—the accident, my parents' leaving, my back hurting—created an environment where one bad decision could lead to many more.

With my parents gone, I started spending huge amounts of time at the tattoo parlor. I had already gotten six tattoos there, but the shop didn't evolve into my hangout until my parents left. There wasn't much to recommend the place, just a bland storefront next to a shady massage parlor, part of the Tampa area's endless strip-mall landscape.

This, somehow, became my home away from home. I sat in the chair and got tattoo after tattoo. Some days I'd get three or four. Some days I'd sit in that chair all day long, feeling the needles mark up my body.

I was troubled; my back kept me off the field, and none of the Devil Rays' doctors could understand what was wrong. They put me through a battery of tests—MRI, CAT scan—and gave me cortisone shots in the area of pain. No test showed anything, and none of the shots helped, which made me more frustrated. I knew what I was feeling, even if the tests didn't agree. The team started to believe I was losing interest, that maybe I didn't want to play.

I settled into a routine. My mornings were spent at the spring training complex, getting treatment for my back and trying to figure out what was wrong. The afternoons were spent in the tattoo parlor.

■ ■ ■

My life had been blessed. I was nineteen, a few months from turning twenty, and I was close enough to the big leagues to spark discussion—and apparently disagreement—within the Devil Rays' organization. From the outside, it looked like a perfect life, my path paved with gold.

The Devil Rays didn't pressure me to produce. If anything, I thought my career could have been accelerated faster than it was. I agreed with Rothschild, of course, because I felt like a big-leaguer and wanted to be a big-leaguer. It seemed like a natural progression. The pressure I felt came from me; I've always expected more of myself than others have.

So what was wrong? Why didn't my life feel as good on the inside as it looked from the outside? To me, the problem was incredibly simple: My back hurt, and nobody knew why. Ever since the accident I couldn't shake the stabbing pain I felt whenever I changed directions quickly or attempted to make an explosive movement.

To that point in my life, I'd never been alone. To that point in my life, I'd never been without baseball. To that point in my life, I'd never been without my parents.

I could sense the doubts from the team about my back, and I began to wonder, too. The pain was there, it was real, but nobody could find anything wrong with me. Doubt started to work its way into my mind, too. Was I imagining it? Did I really want to play baseball?

My mind started to mess with me. My back hurt, but was it real? Were the doctors and coaches who looked at me sideways right?

So maybe it was inevitable that I would find a place outside baseball to hang out. And maybe it was inevitable that once I found a place where I felt I belonged—even if it was a tattoo parlor—I stayed there. It was nonthreatening and comfortable, and nowhere else in my life could I find a place that was both.

The guys in the shop became my friends, I guess, but it seems like I slid into their lives through osmosis. A guy named Kevin did most of the work on me. He would work and I would sit back and we'd talk about pretty much nothing all day long. I didn't have much in common with the guys who worked there. They weren't baseball fans, although they came to know who I was and what I did for a living. They were what you'd expect from guys working at a tattoo parlor, I guess: young and kind of aimless. Kevin had a young son, about three or four at the time, and the little boy was around the margins of life at the shop.

For me, the chair was an escape. I could sit there and escape from baseball and the people who wondered why

I wasn't playing and the whispers that suggested I wasn't really injured and had lost my drive for the game. With my eyes closed and the ink taking shape under my skin, the world got a lot smaller. There were no expectations, nobody telling me how great I was or how great I could be. There was nobody wondering when they were going to see a return on their nearly $4 million investment. If I had been peppered with baseball questions while I sat in the chair I would have found somewhere else to hang out.

The hours I spent inking my body could be seen as self-punishment, maybe even self-mutilation. I'm sure a psychologist would have a field day with that, and several of them tried. Even an amateur could see I was abusing myself on the outside to mask the pain on the inside.

But what caused that interior pain? I'm still not sure, but like everybody, I have my theories. My entire life had been devoted to baseball. I'd been playing since I was old enough to remember, and from the time I turned seven years old people who watched me thought I was destined for the big-leagues. All around me they would whisper, "That's Josh Hamilton; he's going to make it big someday." And not just the big leagues, but big-league stardom. And not just stardom, but superstardom. The idea was never phrased as a question, or delivered as an opinion. It was a given, as certain as the changing of the seasons. I thought the same thing myself, obviously, since I first voiced that intention to my parents when I was twelve years old. I accepted the expectations, even encouraged them, but at some point they began to feel like a burden.

What started as a compliment — "Josh Hamilton, can't-miss prospect" — began to take on a different tone. In my mind, it started to sound like an order. And if I didn't fulfill the order, if I didn't step up to meet and exceed each of the expectations placed upon me, did that by definition make me a failure?

I expressed none of this verbally, of course, because it wasn't something I owned the words to articulate. And who would have understood, or even listened? Were the tattoos a simple backlash against this growing burden, a desire to experience something new, just because I could? Was I changing myself on the outside to reflect the changes I felt on the inside?

It started as a release, a mostly harmless act of rebellion. But after a while, it no longer felt like a release. It felt like confinement, another master to obey.

At this point in my life, at nineteen years old, I was considered the best minor-league player in baseball. My future was a consistent topic of conversation in the Tampa–St. Pete area. Since the team came into existence in 1997, the Rays had done nothing but finish in last place. They lost with young players, and they lost with old players.

The fans wanted something different. Ownership wanted something different. The team looked destined for another hundred-loss season. The roster was filled with a collection of past-their-prime veterans—Greg Vaughn, Vinny Castilla, Fred McGriff—with a few not-ready-for-prime players mixed in. And the pitching staff, like all Rays' pitching staffs since the team was born, was better left undiscussed.

This is where I came in. I was something different. The fans always want the top prospects to be brought up quickly, no matter what the people making the decisions believe is right. On a team like the Devil Rays, there is more pressure to move forward. The number-one pick in the draft—a guy who is rated the top prospect in the game after two minor-league seasons—is seen as someone who should be in a major-league uniform right now, no questions asked.

I was very close to fulfilling my dream and taking a big step toward making everybody's expectations a reality. And yet I was in a state of mental anguish, unsure how to escape. Was the pain a backlash against baseball, against expectation? Was it a fear of failure, or a fear of success?

I started to question myself. I understood where the baseball people were coming from, but I was too young to see the bigger picture. The team was searching for an identity, and it was dying to put guys on the field who might be able to sell tickets and generate excitement even if the team wasn't quite ready to win.

The theme of spring 2001 around the Devil Rays could be described as optimistically defeatist. If the team was going to be bad anyway, why not be bad with young players who could get better and might be fun to watch?

I was the centerpiece of that idea, the number-one pick who could wear the label The Future for now, and The Franchise for later.

I wanted this, too, but it couldn't happen the way my back felt. They put me through another round of MRIs and CAT scans and every other test they could think of, and still they found nothing, and still I told them the pain was too much to bear. I was taking prescription painkillers without much relief. The Devil Rays' frustration was rapidly turning to exasperation, even anger. Was I imagining it? Was my internal pain manifesting itself as physical pain?

Clearly, the designs that kept springing up on my body, working from the top down, were an exterior sign of my interior confusion. In a sense, I became addicted to the feeling of getting tattoos—the first sign of my addictive personality. I almost laugh when people ask me to explain the meaning behind each of my body's twenty-six tattoos. The truth is, most of the time I wasn't interested in what they were putting on my body. Some of the symbols really didn't mean that much to me, and some of them meant nothing at all. The artists were in charge; they'd make suggestions and I'd take a passing glance at what they were going to do and give it a shrugging okay.

I had six tattoos by the time my parents went back to North Carolina. I had more than fifteen by the time they came back.

My momma likes to say she knew things weren't right from the moment she saw the first tattoo. She saw it as an omen. When I walked in the door and she saw the word HAMMER across my right biceps, she closed her eyes tight, as if hoping she could wish it away.

And there were more. There were many more. Blue flames running up my forearms. Various demons on my legs. The devil on the inside of my left elbow. An eyeless demon on my right leg.

I didn't know it at the time, but no eyes is a symbol of a soulless being. And that's exactly what I was on my way to becoming.

When I showed up with tribal signs on my stomach, my mom's reaction was one of anger mixed with disgust.

"What tribe are you from, Josh?"

Her tone was mocking.

When I tried to smile her comment away, she pressed on.

"No, I'm serious, Josh. Tell me what tribe you're from?"

I didn't have any idea what the tribal signs meant. Kevin thought they looked cool, so I let him go. If it bought me some time in the chair, time away from facing the real problems in my life, then I was fine with it. Two or three tattoos in a day, I didn't care. A day spent in the chair meant another day I didn't have to fill.

■　■　■

The reporters covering the Devil Rays tried to find out why I wasn't playing, and the answers they got didn't satisfy them. They wrote about the accident and my back pain, but when they tried to get a diagnosis they were met with shrugs.

I felt pressured to play, so I did. I started swinging a bat and working out in the outfield, and I never felt right. My boastful plan on draft day—three years in the minors fifteen in the majors—veered off course. This was my third year in the minors, and I was sent to Class AA Orlando to start the season. It was a promotion, but this one-step-at-a-time path wasn't what I had in mind.

And then, adding injury to injury, I tore a quad muscle running out a ground ball in the first month of the season. Young, confused, and impatient, I sat around waiting for my leg to heal, and then I ended up back at Class A Charleston on an injury-rehabilitation assignment.

My leg was better, but my back did not improve. Neither did anybody's ability to diagnose it. The pain and the uncertainty showed on the field. My mind wasn't right at any time during this season. I hit .180 in 20 games for Orlando. I had no power and couldn't turn on the ball for fear of hurting my back worse.

I was a lost cause, and baseball started to feel like a job. All of this happened so quickly; I went from being on the fast track in February, when Rothschild told me he thought I was ready for the big leagues, to being stuck in neutral by the middle of May.

As a last resort, the Devil Rays sent me to a back specialist in Los Angeles named Dr. Robert Watkins. He examined me, then gave me an MRI, and right there on the film was a white spot on the spine that he said was a pocket of fluid pushing against a nerve. Dr. Watkins said I was suffering from Par's Defect, which occurs when one of the vertebrae doesn't mature completely. With the trauma from the accident serving as the catalyst, this pocket of fluid had found its way into an opening that would have been covered by a normal-sized vertebra.

There's your pain, he said, pointing to the white spot.

I could have kissed him.

"So I wasn't imagining it," I told him.

"No, it's perfectly real. Now we have to get rid of it. That's the tricky part."

Dr. Watkins said a cortisone shot would remove the pain, but the shot had to be administered to just the right spot. To do that, he had to use a CAT scan to pinpoint the exact location of the fluid sac. When he found it, he plunged the needle into my spine till it felt like it was grinding on bone. But as soon as the needle was removed, the pain was gone. I'd never thanked a man so many times in my life.

I went home to Raleigh to go through rehabilitation. For the first time, I wondered whether I was going to make it to the big leagues. The game had always come so easily to me, and now I was faced with injuries, one after another. The injuries created doubts, and the doubts created a question in my mind: Was all this worth it?

FIVE

MY IDEAL OFF-SEASON would include a couple of months of fishing and hunting followed by two months of working out in preparation for spring training. The house my bonus money bought in Garner, North Carolina, a five-thousand-square-foot colonial ranch house on twenty-two acres with a pond, was the perfect off-season hangout.

But the off-season following my disappointing 2001 season wasn't as much fun as I would have liked. I needed to get my body back in shape to play. I needed to quiet the whispers questioning my toughness and commitment to the game.

I had to make a statement, so after the holidays I left home and went to Bradenton to work out at the Bollitieri Academy, which is run by the IMG agency. My quad was fully healed. My arm felt good and my swing felt good and everything was falling into place. If I could stay healthy—knock on wood—this was going to be the year that answered all the questions and silenced all the doubts.

And then, in keeping with my star-crossed existence of the previous twelve months, I injured my back during training and could barely get out of bed in the morning. I was scheduled to report for spring training in less than two weeks, and there was no way that was going to happen.

When word got back to the Devil Rays, I could sense their disappointment turning to anger.

Here we go again, they thought.

Here I go again, I thought.

■ ■ ■

Depression. Disappointment. Discouragement. Whatever lousy feeling you could imagine, I was feeling it. Once again, troubling thoughts started to drift in and out of my mind. Is this worth it? If I put in all this work to get healthy and still end up getting hurt, what's the point? If my body won't stay together, how can I expect to play a full season and fulfill my dreams?

With no baseball, no parents, and no responsibilities, I returned to the tattoo shop, my default home away from home. My tattoo collection grew from the low teens to about twenty, and once again I spent entire days doing nothing but sitting in a chair watching my skin turn color. I became part of the landscape there, like another piece of furniture. I didn't care how much it cost or how long it took. The longer the better, really.

One weekday I hung out until closing time. Kevin and another artist named Bill were talking about something in a low voice, and when they were finished Kevin came back to the chair and asked me if I wanted to go out after they closed the shop.

I thought about it for less than a second and said sure, that would be great. I was the guy who never went out, not even in high school, and something about going out with these guys seemed exciting and new. They were including me, and it was an indication of how far my self-esteem had fallen that I jumped at the chance to go out with them.

I didn't bother to ask where we were going, or what we were going to do. The particulars didn't matter. With baseball and my parents out of my life temporarily, it was the perfect storm of vulnerability.

Our first stop was a strip club. I walked up to the door trying to act cool. It was a lie, though, because inside I was nervous, trying not to make it obvious that this was something I'd never done before.

Inside the club, one of the guys ordered a round of beers. I drank one, something I'd never done before.

And then I drank several more.

By this time, I was caught up in the scene. This was far outside the realm of my experience, but it didn't take long for me to feel comfortable. Too comfortable. After we left the strip club, we went to Kevin's house. I was in that state of drunkenness where I thought this was the greatest thing in the world, and these guys were my greatest friends in the world. We were all laughing and talking and having a great time.

Baseball and injuries and expectations were the furthest things from my mind.

After we'd settled down for a while with the television and some more booze, someone pulled out a mirror and began to cut up some cocaine. Somewhere inside me an alarm went off, but I ignored it.

I asked them, "What is that?"

I knew, but I'd never seen it before.

"It's cocaine, man."

"What's it make you feel like?"

"It makes you feel jacked up. Try it, you'll see."

I stared at it. I was weak. I couldn't imagine letting

79

these guys down. They had become the most important people in my world.

Or maybe I just didn't care.

Whatever the case, I was in. I leaned over and inhaled a line. I didn't know what to expect, but by the time I'd lifted my head up I knew I liked it. The fog in my brain lifted. I had energy and life. I was a new man.

They looked at me expectantly. I didn't tell them all this was new to me, but they must have known. When they saw the smile on my face, they laughed. They were right—I loved it.

Immediately, the cloud from the alcohol was gone. I was alert and alive and funny and smart. Nothing hurt.

Kevin and Bill were the coolest guys for introducing me to this feeling. We were even better friends now.

It was the worst decision of my life. I knew I shouldn't have done it. I knew I should never do it again.

Inside, though, I knew I would. I knew deep down this was the start of something. It was exciting and exhilarating and terrifying all at the same time.

I've tried to take my mind back to that moment, to unspool history back to the time I was sitting in that chair, to imagine what would have happened if I had said no when they asked me to go out with them. Or even to go back to the moment when the mirror appeared, to say no to that. I've tried to imagine my life if I had simply said I had something else to do. Would it have happened anyway? Would my moment of weakness have come somewhere else, with someone else?

That one decision triggered a series of events that nobody could ever have imagined. So many lives changed in the wake of that decision.

I considered myself a Christian at this stage of my life.

I had always been a Christian, but I had given it more thought since the night in Princeton, West Virginia, when I saw the face of the devil and the face of Jesus on the same night.

Those visions prompted me to seek a greater understanding of what it means to be a Christian, and a month after my first professional season ended I went to my uncle Joe and aunt Mary's house to have a serious discussion about Jesus's role in my life. My aunt and uncle were always the strongest religious presences in my life; when we went to church on Sundays, they were the ones who provided the push.

So it was natural for me to seek them out as I sought answers. Sitting in their living room, discussing what it means to accept the Lord, I felt His presence in the room. Uncle Joe and Aunt Mary felt it, too, and asked me, "Do you accept Jesus Christ as your Lord and Savior?"

"I do," I said.

And I did. I was saved that night, and what I felt in that room was real. For whatever reason, though, I didn't have the tools or the motivation to follow through. I wasn't doing the things I needed to do to be a good Christian, and I left myself open to temptation. The devil comes at you a thousand times harder when you're a child of God, and he came at me with his best stuff.

From the moment I tried cocaine, I became a different person. I wasn't playing baseball, but this—this was the surge of adrenaline I got from hitting a ball 450 feet with the game on the line. With this, I was smart and strong and invincible. I was someone else. Gone was the guy who lived for baseball and family. Gone was the guy who didn't go to the prom in high school because he was afraid of being around people who might put him in a compromising position and jeopardize his career. Gone was the guy who went with his brother and his daddy and his momma to take batting practice just hours after being picked as the number-one player in the draft.

Maybe that guy was drifting away from me anyway, and this was simply my logical destination after a series of wrong turns. Maybe it started with the accident, or the independence, or the tattoos. Who would ever know?

I've always been able to get along with all different types of people. I always wanted everyone to be happy, and I always tried to see the good in everybody. I could hang with Ashley Pittman or Carl Crawford or, as I now knew, Kevin and Bill. This was the way I was raised—to see the good in people—and it was no different when my crowd changed from baseball players to drug users. That had always been a positive aspect of my personality, but now it seemed more like naïveté than acceptance.

Regardless, the tattoo guys were my circle of friends now, and I worked to make sure they liked me. They weren't bad people; they just did bad things. I brought them a couple of my signed Devil Rays jerseys, even though they weren't baseball fans. We were tight.

Whether the choice to use was an impulsive, random decision or the culmination of a series of poor choices, the result was the same. From the moment I tried cocaine, I became the coke-sniffing baseball player. I was a guy who was in violation of my contract, a guy who was willing to take a huge chance with his talent and his career, a guy who was willing to trade everything he'd achieved for temporary acceptance from a bunch of guys he didn't really know.

On that one night, with that one moment of weakness, I made a decision that will stay with me the rest of my life.

I believe the seeds of addiction were planted that night, and my fate was preordained from the moment I decided to leave the tattoo shop with Kevin and Bill. With that one decision, I embarked on a journey that took me to a place I never could have imagined, where nothing else in life mattered as much as that drug.

Because I didn't stop drinking and doing cocaine. The buzz of that drug lingered. I did not go out the next day and use, and I didn't allow it to rule my life until much later. But it did stay with me. Two days later I used, and using became a recreational thing from that point forward. Every other night, maybe two nights in a row—hey, I had money and time and opportunity. Why not? There was no one around to stop me.

The events of that first adventure with the guys from the tattoo shop led to more. Being around these guys made it easier to forget about baseball and easier to keep from doing the things I needed to do to get my head and body right to get back to playing the game.

I drifted further and further from being the person I needed to be. I became a case study of my theory of people, places, and things. Now that I can see my own gradual deterioration with a clear eye, I speak to groups about this: If you hang out with a group of people in a certain place, you're bound to end up doing the things they do.

I can't count the number of times someone said, either in the media or to someone in my family, "If it could happen to Josh Hamilton, it could happen to anybody."

That doesn't make it better, and it certainly isn't an excuse. Nobody pushed me or forced me. I walked out of the tattoo shop with Kevin and Bill. I walked into the strip club. I leaned over the mirror and inhaled the cocaine into my system.

But I believe if it could happen to me it could happen to anybody. I believe I am a good person who made bad choices. I believe I am living testimony to the power of addiction.

I'm the cautionary tale. I accept that.

SIX

ONE OF THE LAST TATTOOS I got is on my right calf. I chose this one myself, but I don't know why. There was no rhyme or reason behind the choice, any more than any of the others.

It's a picture of Jesus's face superimposed over a cross. He's on the same leg with the demon with no eyes.

When I look at myself now, I see what I couldn't see then. This was spiritual warfare, taking place subconsciously on my body.

The soulless demon.

The face of Jesus.

The battle had begun.

SEVEN

TWO WEEKS to the day after I used cocaine for the first time, a member of the Devil Rays' Employee Assistance Program told me the team wanted me to see a sports psychologist.

"Okay," I said. "Why?"

"The team's concerned about your injuries, and we'd like you to talk to someone about them," he said. "Everyone just wants to make sure you're okay. This'll be good, just someone to talk to."

Two years of injuries had taken their toll on me. The back problem that started with the accident, the quad, now the back again... yeah, I was frustrated. The team was frustrated, too. I assume there was a meeting among the top brass and the familiar subjects were discussed: whether I was really hurt, whether I really wanted to play, whether the problem was in my head and not my back.

The first step to a solution, according to them, was a psychologist.

The psychologist was employed by the team. I was a little hesitant to go see him, but once I started talking to him I found I liked him. We spoke about my injuries, and what it felt like to know you can play at a higher level than your body will allow. We talked about expectations—my own as well as the team's—and he caught on pretty quickly to the idea that I'm my own worst critic.

He listened and I talked. It was pleasant enough, but I wasn't entirely sure how it was going to make my back feel better to talk to him about it. As the conversation started to die down, we both sat there awkwardly until he finally asked, "Well, is there anything else bothering you? Anything else you want to talk about?"

I could have said no, shook his hand and left the office. It would have been that easy. Instead, I sat and thought about it for a minute. I ran it through my mind at warp speed, over and over: Should I? Should I trust him, or should I leave?

I stayed in the chair.

What if I had gotten up and left? How different would my life have been?

"There is something," I said.

"Yes…"

"The last couple of weeks…well…I've kind of been experimenting with drugs."

No shock registered on his face. He retained his professional detachment and asked the normal questions—which drugs, how often, with whom. I had used cocaine with the tattoo guys seven or eight times—roughly every other day—to this point. I continued to like it, and I saw no real reason to stop. Since I wasn't playing, I wasn't concerned that it might hurt my ability to play. I liked it, and I liked how it let me enter a different world and forget my problems.

He nodded politely to keep me talking. He didn't act judgmental. We talked about the set of circumstances—frustration with injury, boredom, loneliness—that led me to make such a flawed decision.

I don't know where I expected this discussion to lead. I knew he worked for the team, but I believed it was a confidential doctor-patient conversation.

My decision to bring up the issue showed how conflicted I was. As I was making my confession, it didn't seem real to me. It felt as if I was talking about someone else, describing someone else's life. Experimenting with drugs? This couldn't be me.

■　■　■

The focus of drugs in baseball had shifted from the cocaine era of the 1980s to the performance-enhancing era of the past decade. In 2001, MLB unilaterally implemented its first random drug-testing program for minor-leaguers. All players outside the forty-man roster were subject to testing for "steroid-based, performance-enhancing drugs, plus drugs of abuse (marijuana, cocaine)."

Steroids never interested me. I would wonder at times how much better I could be if I did them—mostly when I saw someone less talented tearing it up with the extra help—but I was never tempted to do them. Strange as it sounds coming from me, I thought taking performance-enhancing drugs would cheat the game. I had always been taught to respect the game, and whenever the topic of steroids came up, my daddy would say, "If you can hit the ball five hundred feet and the fences are four hundred feet away, why do you need to hit it any farther? And if you can throw the ball from the outfield fence to home plate, why do you need to throw it any farther?"

The strength of the Major League Players Association made the minor leagues the first battleground in the drug war. The first positive test carried a fifteen-game suspension, the second thirty, the third sixty, and the fourth a full year. A fifth offense called for a lifetime ban from professional baseball.

■ ■ ■

The morning after I met with the psychologist I received a call from the same EAP employee who had arranged the appointment.

"Josh, we're sending you to the Betty Ford Center for rehab," he said.

His words took my breath away. Rehab? You mean drug rehab? The doctor turned me in? He went right back to the Devil Rays and told them what I confided. I couldn't speak, but my mind raced.

I couldn't keep this secret. People will find out. I'll have to tell my family. This will follow me wherever I go.

He kept talking, but I wasn't really listening. Something about leaving tomorrow, a plane, thirty days in treatment, the best thing for me, get my head straight, come back ready to play.

I didn't really know what to say, but I blurted out something that probably made no sense. I was in shock. I had no idea how that conversation had led to this. I had tried cocaine seven or eight times, and now I was branded an addict? I was going to Betty Ford?

I hadn't failed a test. I had simply confided in a professional. I hung up the phone and tried to make sense of the past twenty-four hours. Right there in the drug policy are the words, "The EAP director will arrange for an appropriate and confidential medical evaluation of the individual, and will assist in prescribing the appropriate treatment, counseling, and after care."

I've often thought about that episode—how it happened, whether it was right, if I should have questioned the confidentiality aspect of my conversation. I always come back to the same answer: It needed to happen that way. The script was being written somewhere else, and even though the sequence made no sense to me or anyone around me, it made sense to someone somewhere.

That night, I made the toughest call of my life. I punched in my parents' number back in Garner, took a deep breath, and prepared myself for the worst. I closed my eyes as it rang, wanting to hang up but knowing I couldn't. My daddy answered. We made small talk for a few seconds, but there was no hiding my mood. Daddy knew there was something going on, so I stopped trying to pretend otherwise.

"I'm going away for a while tomorrow," I said.

"Okay. What for? Your back?"

"No, the team's sending me to Betty Ford."

No response. The silence was thick as he tried to digest the information.

"What? Wait, what are you talking about, Josh?"

I could hear my momma in the background, reacting to his disbelief. He held the phone away from his ear for a second and said, "They're sending Josh to Betty Ford."

"Betty *Ford*?" she asked. "The *rehab* place?"

I sat there, in an empty apartment in Florida, listening to this drama play out in the big house in North Carolina. They were shocked, angry, confused, but there had been signs. The tattoos, the injuries, the time away from the game—believing I was a drug user didn't take the huge leap it would have just two years earlier.

Feeling the need to fill the silence, I said, "They sent me to talk to someone about my injuries and I told him

I've been experimenting with drugs. They called me back and told me I'm going to Betty Ford."

They were helpless. They didn't understand. Nobody did, least of all me. They wanted to come down, but I was leaving the next day. They wanted to go with me, but they knew they couldn't. They wanted to rewind and start over, figure out how to keep this from happening in the first place, but that was impossible.

They didn't want to hang up, but there was nothing left to say.

EIGHT

THE DRIVER PICKED ME UP at the airport and drove me through the desert and past the rows of palm trees to the front of the famous Betty Ford Clinic, a sprawling single-story white complex in Rancho Mirage. I walked through the doors that had opened for hundreds, maybe thousands of well-known people seeking to reassemble their lives.

This whole trip was a shock to me. I didn't know what to expect, and I didn't really know why I was there. I was met at the desk by an intake coordinator, who gave me a quick tour of the facility—dining room, meeting rooms, all very nice—before showing me to my room and introducing me to my roommate. I shook his hand but the name filtered in and out without registering. I wasn't interested.

I walked around in a daze, looking and nodding but not really hearing or seeing. It felt like I was living somebody else's life.

I didn't associate myself with addicts, and that was the first issue wrestling around in my mind. I'd used maybe seven or eight times to that point, and now I was about to hear that I was powerless in the face of my addiction and all that other stuff. It just didn't compute.

The label *addict* had been attached to me just the day before, and sitting there in my room with a suitcase at my feet gave me some time to sort through the events of the last twenty-four hours. My attitude began to change from one of straight confusion to one of anger. I didn't know why the Devil Rays would unilaterally decide to ship me off to a treatment center, where the label was affixed permanently.

I didn't believe I was an addict, but here I was. I didn't associate myself with any of the people here, but here I was. This would be my home for the next thirty days.

The first step was to be interviewed by a therapist. When he used the word *addict,* I was ready. I immediately challenged him.

"I'm not an addict," I said.

He sat there calmly, like he was dealing with a child. He said something about denial and then repeated the word: *addict.*

"I've used about eight times, and you're telling me I'm an addict?"

He looked at me and didn't say anything. His patronizing manner made me angry.

"You're an idiot," I said.

The exchange set the tone. In group sessions they made us talk about ourselves and our problems. I cooperated to an extent, but as soon as they heard my story they felt they had the answer. The circumstances that led to my presence here made me confrontational, and their packaged conclusions made it worse.

I folded my arms across my chest and vowed not to cooperate. Everyone here was an expert, and it was all so easy: My parents had suffocated me; they were overprotective; they didn't give me room to breathe, so it was natural that I would rebel.

It was so obvious anybody could see it.

I disagreed. This was garbage, but it was predictable garbage. It was the same garbage I'd been hearing since I started out in the minor leagues.

"Whatever I did, I did myself," I said whenever silence wasn't an option. "My parents didn't have anything to do with it. They didn't cause this."

Nobody heard me. Everything I said was twisted back toward the idea that I was living in denial. I felt trapped, like the walls were closing in. I either had to agree with them or be told I was in denial. There was no other right answer.

In fact, from the moment I told the sports psychologist I'd experimented with drugs, the answers had been decided for me: 1) I was an addict, and 2) my parents caused it.

I got pissed off. I got quieter with each passing day. I seethed. I didn't speak to my roommate and I tried not to make eye contact. I didn't want to be there and I didn't hide my feelings. I spent more and more time with earphones in place, listening to music and tuning out the world.

By the fourth day, I was uncooperative in the meetings. I sat there and let everyone tell their stories and work out their problems while I stared off into space. All this therapy seemed pointless, someone else's problem. I needed to get healthy and get back on the baseball field, that's all. I'd done cocaine a few times, big deal. I was still alive, and I wasn't an addict, and nobody really needed to know my business, anyway.

My increasing noncompliance was noted by the people in charge, I'm sure, and it only cemented their views that I was in dire need of help. At this point, I wasn't buying into the idea of myself as addict, no matter where I was or how many times someone tried to attach the label.

On my eighth day at Betty Ford, during a break from group, I walked back to my room, packed up my stuff, and walked out the door. I couldn't take it anymore. I didn't acknowledge anyone or say good-bye, and nobody tried to stop me.

I called a cab to take me to a hotel, where I used my credit card—one of the few possessions I brought from Florida—to secure the room. I turned on the television and tried to decompress. I made no attempt to understand what I'd just been through, probably because I had yet to understand the actions that brought me to this point in the first place.

After a while, I picked up the phone and dialed the house in Garner. I knew my parents had just purchased two plane tickets to fly out to attend the "Family Days" portion of the treatment program, and I winced when I considered what would go through their minds when I told them the latest turn my story had taken.

"Hey, Daddy," I said when he answered. "I need to come home."

Just when they thought their minds couldn't spin any faster...

First, they were introduced to my drug use—at that point, my *limited* drug use—when I called and told them I was heading for Betty Ford. Then, just as they make some sense of this information and decide to come out to support me through the treatment, they get a call from me telling them I'm coming home after eight days.

They didn't know what to believe or what to tell me.

On the phone, my daddy stammered and said, "I don't understand. I thought you had to stay."

"I just can't take it anymore," I said. "I can't stay here, so I'm coming home."

He didn't know what to say, so he said he'd be there to pick me up at the airport. I could practically hear him shaking his head.

■ ■ ■

Word traveled back to Raleigh in whispers and raised eyebrows. First it was the tattoos: *I hear Josh Hamilton is covered in tattoos.* And then the drugs: *You're not going to believe this, but they're saying Josh Hamilton is doing drugs.*

■ ■ ■

I left Betty Ford, flew back to Raleigh, and then returned to spring training. The Devil Rays didn't ask too many questions, and I didn't offer too many answers. In a strange way, I think the eight-day break from baseball gave my back the time it needed to quiet down and feel better.

When we broke camp, I was sent to Class A Bakersfield in the California League. My career was treading water. The year before, when I was nineteen, Larry Rothschild had told me he would have kept me on the big-league roster if it had been up to him. Now, a year and one trip to rehab later, I was starting my third straight year in Class A ball.

The California League is considered high A ball, but still. The number-one pick—the guy chosen one-one—should be far beyond A ball by his twenty-first birthday.

The meteoric rise I had predicted on the day I was drafted was officially out of the question. This was my fourth year as a pro, and instead of becoming a big-league All-Star I was closer to becoming a major disappointment, both personally and professionally.

I went to Bakersfield on my own. I drifted from my parents, as might be expected, and I got myself an apartment near the ballpark and set out to put my career back on track.

There were enough signs I could still play. During a night game in Bakersfield, I hit a ball that left my bat with such force that it startled me. It rose through the minor-league lights and the Bakersfield moths and kept right on going, over the right-field fence and clear out of the stadium.

When the ball left my bat, it sounded as if every fan in the stands had been punched in the gut at the same time. It was the sound of amazement.

Beyond the right-field fence was a levee running beside the Kern River. The team sent someone out to find the ball, to see if they could measure the blast, and the person who tracked it down found the ball had buried itself in the levee, a couple inches deep in the soft dirt.

They measured it the next day: 549 feet.

The longest home run in history, or at least the longest one anyone ever measured, was hit by Mickey Mantle, the man with whom I had frequently been compared as a high school player. Mantle's blast was measured at 565 feet.

■ ■ ■

There was another momentous event in Bakersfield: For the first time, I used drugs during a baseball season.

We had an off-day. I got up late in the morning, ate something, and then went for a drive. I stopped at a bar and told myself I'd go in and have one, maybe two, drinks. It's a story as old as time: the addict, making a deal with himself he knows he won't be able to keep.

I had developed a liking for Crown Royal. It was my drink of choice, and I could drink the hell out of some Crown. Sometimes a fifth a day, sometimes more. I chatted up the bartender and spent the afternoon in there, drinking Crown and talking.

As night fell, I started to feel drunk and slow. Instead of kicking myself for my stupidity and calling a cab to take me back to my apartment, I asked the bartender if he knew where I could score some coke.

Of course he did.

Sure enough, one phone call and ten minutes later, I was in possession of an eight-ball. I wasn't surprised this transaction happened so quickly and easily; the surprise would have been if it didn't.

I did a little cocaine with my connection to commemorate our new relationship. He also worked as a security guard and had to make his rounds. Since I didn't have anything better to do, I made them with him. Over and over, throughout the night, I walked the perimeter of a building with a stranger, stopping occasionally to do more coke.

I can't remember a thing the guard and I talked about that night—I'm sure none of it was important—but I can close my eyes and see that building and the parking lot. I can feel the aimless sadness of one in an endless string of wasted nights.

There was no sleep for me that night. I went back to the apartment at some point the next morning, wired to the heavens. I checked to see what I had left, and I figured I had enough coke to get me through the next couple of days. We had a game that night, though, and I began to panic about getting my mind straight in time to make it to the ballpark.

When I got to the clubhouse, I was still hyped, but

my strongest emotion was fear. I was afraid that someone would find out. I got dressed, aware of my heart thumping in my chest. Too fast, I thought, and definitely too hard. How was I going to calm myself in time to get loose and play hard without killing myself?

By the time batting practice started, I was honestly afraid I might die on the field. My heart was still hammering like a bass drum, which made any exertion seem dangerous.

As I did my pregame sprints, I prayed my heart wouldn't just race out of my chest. Stopping wasn't an option, though, because I firmly believed any change in the regular routine would raise suspicions. I could see the progression—discovery, hand-wringing, another trip to rehab, another tough call to my parents.

The psychologist was right: The $4 million bonus baby was a drug addict.

I stood in the outfield that night, thinking, "I will never, ever do this again." I went through my get-me-out-of-this-foxhole prayers—Jesus, if you let me pull through this, I'll never do this again. I saw the error of my ways, and I would never do this again. Not in a million years. I made deals, promises, vows.

The next day I needed a line or two, just to get me through the day.

■ ■ ■

Oft-injured. Troubled. These were the adjectives that began attaching themselves to my name like leeches. It was always written that I was "the former number-one pick" in a manner that dripped with disappointment.

It was hard to argue. My 2002 season ended after just fifty-six games in Class A Bakersfield. This time it was my elbow, which began hurting about a month into the season and grew progressively worse until the doctors decided I needed to shut it down. This time, the MRI showed the problem immediately, and the Devil Rays sent me to Birmingham, Alabama, to see Dr. James Andrews, a famous orthopedic surgeon, who cleaned up bone chips in my elbow.

I came home to Garner and hung out, idling away the days. I met up with a guy from high school named Wayne, and we started hanging out pretty much every day. People would see me with Wayne and look at me funny; he was not someone I had hung out with in high school at all. In the high school world of labels—jock, geek, stoner—he was at one end of the spectrum and I was at the other.

I could read the faces of those who had known me for a long time. When they saw me with Wayne their thoughts were so obvious they could have been printed on their foreheads. *Everything they're saying about Josh must be true.*

At this point, I wasn't sure who I was, or who I should be hanging out with. My sense of self was gradually eroding, so maybe it wasn't that unusual that I gravitated toward someone who wasn't at all like me. Wayne was a guy with no direction in high school, and he was a guy with no direction when we started hanging out. In that sense, given my growing aimlessness, maybe we were perfect.

I was still the Devil Rays' property, and when my elbow started healing they sent me to Durham, right down the road, to rehab with the Triple A Durham Bulls. I dressed for games and worked out during the day, but I never played for the Bulls. I wasn't officially a member of the team, but the Devil Rays thought it would be the perfect place to keep an eye on me and also allow me to stay at home.

Even though I wasn't playing, I was still subject to the same rules as any other minor-leaguer, which meant I was subject to random drug testing. And one day before a game in Durham I was given a cup by a drug tester and told to pee while he watched.

My cocaine use was nearly every day, but I peed in the cup with the confidence of a man who had yet to realize the extent of his problem. I wasn't panicked or nervous; I was untouchable.

Bill Evers was the manager of the Bulls, and he called me into his office a few days later. He brought me in, closed the door, and said, "Josh, we got a failed test."

"What? Of mine?"

"Yes, yours."

And so, with that, I entered into Major League Baseball's drug treatment program. I would be subject to stricter testing and a fifteen-game ban from playing. Since I wasn't on an active roster, that didn't matter much to me.

In fact, I was remarkably unaffected by the whole thing. I convinced myself it wasn't real, that I didn't fail a test. It must have been a false positive or some other mistake. Maybe they got my sample mixed up with that of somebody else, a real drug user.

That must have been it.

It couldn't have been me.

■ ■ ■

Wayne thought it was a big deal to hang out with me. I don't like to say that because it sounds conceited, but it was true. Wayne got some mileage out of hanging out with Josh Hamilton, especially since nobody would have ever suspected it was possible.

It didn't take long for our relationship to center on drugs. Wayne served a purpose for me—I could send him out to get the stuff and have him hold it for me. I always felt cleaner and less guilty if I wasn't the one driving out to buy it, or the one holding it. I had to watch myself. At this stage, with baseball still in the picture, it felt like less of a problem—less real—if I could just sit back and use the stuff when it was presented to me without having to do the dirty work.

One day in August I had seen a high school classmate of ours named Katie Chadwick. She was a pretty single mom with a daughter about eighteen months old. Katie and I knew each other in high school, but we weren't really friends. She was not a baseball fan and never saw me play, and she was unimpressed and mostly unmoved by the Josh Hamilton Phenomenon that swept through Athens Drive High School during my senior year.

When her friends were walking around the hallways with baseballs for me to sign, she asked them, "What are y'all doing? Is that something I should be doing?"

But when I saw her this time, I told Wayne I wouldn't mind getting to know her better, and before I knew it he was on the phone to her.

"Katie, I've got Josh Hamilton here, and he wants to meet you."

For Katie, this was confusing on many levels. She wasn't a friend of either of us in high school, and now she was being asked to digest a bunch of conflicting information. First, it was hard for her to get her mind around the idea that I was even associating with Wayne. She didn't know me that well in high school, but she knew me well enough to know I didn't hang out with guys like Wayne. Second, she didn't know whether to believe I really wanted to meet her, because we had had no contact since high school and the only things she knew about me were from the newspaper reports of my baseball career.

She agreed to meet with me, anyway, and we began dating. I immediately fell in love with Julia, Katie's daughter, and I used to change her diaper and play with her all the time. Katie and I got along well, but she soon discovered that her suspicions were correct: If I was hanging out with Wayne, I must be using drugs.

After four or five months, we broke up. My drug use was the big factor in ending our relationship. There were times when using and hanging out with Wayne and some other hangers-on was more important to me than being with Katie, and that wasn't what she had in mind for our relationship.

Katie's father, Michael Dean Chadwick, was a recovering addict who grew up in Baltimore selling and using crack on the streets. He was a remarkable success story, having overcome his past to become one of the most respected and successful homebuilders and developers in the Raleigh area. Katie's mother, Janice, stayed with Michael and helped him beat his addiction. The Chadwicks also drew on their faith to get them through the tragic death of Katie's little brother, nine-year-old Mikey, who was killed in an automobile accident. Katie's dad told the family's story at local churches, and his speeches were dynamic and motivational.

Katie understood addiction, but that didn't mean she was willing to accept whatever I threw at her. We liked each other, and we got along great, but this one thing stood between us, prying us apart.

NINE

THE LAST PLACE I should have been during February 2003 was at a major-league spring training. I was a mess, using every day, growing increasingly paranoid and defensive, listening to nobody. And yet there I was, at the Devil Rays' spring training complex in St. Petersburg, trying to hide my addiction and make the ballclub.

The second half of that statement is debatable. My first drug suspension was over, but I don't know how hard I tried to make the club, or even whether it was a possibility. My head wasn't in it, and my heart followed.

The Rays made a big move before the 2003 season, bringing Lou Piniella out of retirement to manage the team. Lou was known as an old-school hardass, the kind of guy who flourished working for George Steinbrenner and the Yankees. He was going to usher in a new era of Rays' baseball, where guys played hard and were held accountable, and failure would no longer be seen as a by-product of wearing the uniform.

To me, it didn't really matter. Drugs had taken over. They'd gone from a recreational mistake, something I stupidly thought I could control or ignore or deny, to a full-blown personal disaster. It was astonishing and perfectly natural how quickly drugs and the drug culture had taken up residence in my life.

By the time spring training started, I had cocaine with me nearly all the time. It was with me at my apartment, but I couldn't leave it there when I left for the ballpark in the morning because I might need it. I couldn't leave it in my truck in the players' parking lot; I was too worried about what might happen if someone either saw it or broke into my truck and found it.

The cocaine would stay in the pocket of my pants, I decided. Inside the pants, it would stay on a hook hanging inside my locker while I took the field. Freaked, I would spend my whole time on the field worried the clubbie might go into my locker to hang something up and accidentally knock the pants off the hook, spilling a vial of cocaine all over the clubhouse floor and exposing my secret for the world to see.

While I was in the shower, I worried that one of my teammates might reach into my locker for some deodorant or toothpaste and inadvertently catch a finger on my belt loop and upend my pants, spilling a vial of cocaine all over the clubhouse floor and exposing my secret for all the world to see.

It wasn't rational, but nothing about me was rational.

Baseball wasn't fun. I was on guard all the time, protecting my secret. I avoided people, even teammates who had been my friends, like Carl Crawford. I couldn't see people for who they were; I saw only the reflection of me I could see in their looks and behavior. I couldn't relax to save my life.

Carl and I share a business manager, Steve Reed, and early in spring training Carl called Steve and asked him what was up with me.

Steve said, "Nothing as far as I know. Why?"

"I don't know, man," Carl said. "Your boy's changed. You might want to see what's up with him, because he's tense and edgy all the time. Guys are wondering what happened."

Not surprisingly, my play on the field was erratic. I'd have days where I felt like the old Josh, ripping balls over the fence in batting practice and doing all the things that made me one of baseball's top prospects. But most of the time my mind drifted and I played like a guy who had lost interest. I struggled to do things I used to be able to do in my sleep. I could hide the cocaine in my pants pocket, but I couldn't hide its effects. I was sick, and that was impossible to hide.

During the second week of spring training, I stayed up most of the night, went to sleep around 5:00 A.M. and didn't wake up in time to get to the ballpark in time. I was about an hour late, and in spring training nobody—and I mean *nobody*—shows up late.

On my drive in to the ballpark from home, I settled on a story: car trouble. Not very imaginative, I know, but that's not the point. The point is, I convinced myself it was true. I repeated it for twenty minutes on the drive, and by the time I parked in the players' lot and walked into the clubhouse, it was no longer a story. It was the truth.

Besides, I couldn't tell Lou that I was out all night and couldn't get up in time to be at the ballpark by eight-thirty. My behavior in the first two weeks of spring training had already caught the attention of the team and Piniella. I couldn't just hand over the evidence.

I told Lou my story and he just looked at me and said, "Okay, don't let it happen again."

Two days after, I was late again. This time I drove to

the park perfecting a story about my alarm clock. I walked in with a sheepish look on my face and muttered something about oversleeping. This time Lou just looked at me and nodded.

My ability to concoct stories and convince myself they were true was the same ability that allowed me to deny a positive drug test. At some level of my soul, I still couldn't come to terms with my drug use. The truth was too hard to face, so I denied tests and made up excuses and somehow convinced myself I could believe both.

The team was aware of my problems, and they were trying to put rules in place that might keep me from creating more problems for myself. Since most of my problems occurred in Bradenton, the team forbade me to cross the bridge between Tampa and Bradenton.

That didn't last. I went across the bridge one day during spring training and decided not to come back. I hung out and used and forgot about baseball. No lies about car trouble, no oversleeping, no worries about the clubbie discovering cocaine in the jeans hanging in my locker.

For four days, I stayed gone. I slept when I felt like it, which wasn't often. I didn't answer the phone or make any calls or read the newspapers. No excuses, just AWOL.

At the end of the fourth day, I made a phone call to Devil Rays' general manager, Chuck Lamar.

After being patched through to his office, I said, "Mr. Lamar, Josh Hamilton."

I could feel the disappointment in his voice. They were starting to wonder if I would ever fulfill my promise, if they would ever get a return on their investment. I had my doubts, too.

Mr. Lamar came up with a plan. I would take a ten-day leave of absence. The team would announce it was for personal reasons. This leave would take me through the end of spring training, and I would report to Double A Orlando when the leave ended. I would go home to Garner, gather my thoughts, and return ready to play.

It sounded better than anything I could come up with. I agreed and apologized.

Back home in Garner I sat in the big house on twenty-two acres, the house and land bought on the promise of my baseball talent, and wondered where this would go next. I was scared, sick, and paranoid. I didn't want to hear from anybody, and I wouldn't listen if I did. If I've learned anything, it's that stubbornness is a great way to hide weakness.

I kept using. Ten days at home, with nothing to do but fish in the pond out back and ponder the future, wasn't going to fix anything. It got me out of the team's way, but it wasn't meant to fix anything. That was my job, and I wasn't willing to sign on.

My parents knew, but they couldn't reach me. Nothing worked.

After the personal leave, I was sent to Double A Orlando. Because of my previous failed drug test, I was in the program and subject to regular testing. I had been told I would be tested the day I showed up in Orlando, and still I used that day and showed up at the ballpark knowing I would fail that day's test.

And so, on the afternoon of May 14, 2003, the drug tester brought me the cup and stood by to watch and make sure it was my urine that ended up in it. My heart racing and my mind surprisingly dead to the world, I peed in the cup, watching the stream carry my career away with it.

This would mean a suspension of thirty games. And after that, I would be subject to more testing and more severe penalties. This didn't feel like a temporary disruption—another in a long line of them—as much as a conclusion. This felt like the end, the final straw, the last act of self-destruction.

I put on my uniform, thinking it might be the last time. I went through the motions of pregame warmups, but since I wasn't in the lineup I didn't overexert myself. When the game started, I sat next to hitting coach Steve Henderson, a former big-leaguer and a good man. I trusted Hendu, and seeing him made me realize I had let good people down. I was staring out at the field, trying to keep my mind on the present, trying to calm the frantic beating of my heart.

The scene before me was so familiar, and normally so comforting. The geometry of the game—the baselines, the batter's box, the distance between bases. This was home for me, and playing the game was the one thing I could do better than anyone I knew.

This time, I felt like I was seeing it in the past tense.

I said nothing. I tried swallowing back the burning at the back of my throat, determined not to let it escalate. I couldn't do it. The burning became shudders I couldn't stifle, and then tears I couldn't stop.

Nothing made sense. It didn't make sense that I would knowingly sabotage my career and then sit there and cry about it. I was so deep into this I couldn't find myself. Henderson looked at me. I could feel his eyes on me, and without taking my eyes off the pitcher, I took a deep breath and said, "I think this might be the last time I ever do this."

He didn't ask me why. I assumed he knew. He just told me forever is a long time, that maybe I just need some time to get my head and my priorities straight. I nodded, but I didn't know if I believed him.

After the game I stood at my locker taking off my uniform. The shirt, the pants, the socks—I lingered over every single scrap of clothing, thinking I'd never wear a baseball uniform again.

I hadn't played a game since July 10, 2002, ten months ago.

I might not play another one for a long, long time.

The next day, May 15, 2003, the team announced I was suspended for violating the substance-abuse policy. Untethered, with no job and no responsibilities, I left Florida and went back home.

TEN

PETE LIVED IN a run-down two-story duplex. Wayne found Pete, and he became our dealer and, I guess, our friend. I didn't really have friends; they were more like humans who served as means to an end. That end, increasingly, was cocaine.

I would go down to Pete's house just about every day to buy. I preferred to buy in small amounts, which meant I had to buy more often, which meant I was leaving myself open to being seen more often. And at the same time, I became intensely paranoid about being caught.

My actions didn't make much sense. That came with the territory. I drove a Jaguar XKG with JOSH 22 license plates. I didn't really have a pattern. I didn't have a job or a daily routine or anything resembling a structured life. There were times I would show up at Pete's house and spend hours doing blow and playing video games in the small upstairs loft. There were other times when I would show up at the door, pay my money, get the drugs, and be back in the Jag in less than a minute.

I could fool myself into thinking this was freedom. In reality, I was trapped. The addiction was growing, and the paranoia grew with it. I was addicted not only to the feeling the drug produced, but also to the pursuit and the secrecy involved in getting it.

My frequent trips to Pete's house worried me, so I began altering my driving route to avoid detection. Like a CIA operative dropping a tail, I would drive miles out of the way to get to his house, all in the name of avoiding some unseen—and nonexistent—follower. The location of the house reduced the number of ways I could approach it. But I did my best to vary the routes I took to get there.

The other option was to send someone else. This worked for me, too. I had some friends—or people I thought were friends—who would come over and get the money and bring me drugs in return. I paid these guys something for their time, either in money or product.

Which brings me to another habit I developed: I began to overpay for drugs. In my twisted mind, this was a good business decision. Maybe this was my last hope of retaining my status as the guy who signed for $4 million out of high school. I had been reduced to this: I wanted to be liked, and what better way to be liked than to let Pete keep an extra twenty bucks for his services? You can trace this mentality back to the tattoo shop, where I made bad decisions in the interest of making or keeping what I mistakenly thought were friends.

The overpayments were also down payments on future bad times. The addict's mind is always thinking ahead, perhaps understanding things will always get worse. If I overpaid now, I figured they'd cut me some slack if the time came when I needed to use but didn't have enough money to support the habit.

Whatever the case, I had money when I was dealing with Pete, and he was always happy to see me. No wonder.

It's funny that I cared enough about what a drug dealer

thought of me that I overpaid for drugs, because I didn't care a whole lot for the people in my life who truly loved me and cared for me. And I certainly didn't have enough regard for myself to step back and see how people in the community saw me.

I was buying and using drugs on a regular basis not more than a mile from the high school baseball fields where so many people had watched me play. Fathers would bring their sons to watch me play ball there. Scouts and media people from all over the country came to shake their heads in wonder at my abilities on that field. My senior year I signed autographs between classes while walking down those halls.

And now? Now those memories were starting to fade and I was becoming known as a big waste of talent, a guy who had so much potential but somehow lost his way. Somewhere in the back of my mind I was still a baseball player, but that was receding with every passing day. After the latest suspension, I went six months without picking up a bat or a ball. I didn't feel anything when I drove past the high school field. The focus of my life had shifted, and now I was a guy who overpaid a dealer for drugs so he could stay on his good side and maybe call in some chips when things got worse down the line.

The paranoia extended to everything I did. I was never much of a social user, but as I fell deeper and deeper into addiction I became more solitary. I never went to clubs for fear of being seen and arrested. I spent most of my time in my room in the big house in Garner, avoiding my parents and using.

This retreat into my own world understandably bothered my parents. They didn't know what to do. They'd hear people in the community discussing me, and many of those people insisted on blaming them for my problems. It was the same old story: *They were overprotective parents. They didn't let me breathe. They should have stayed home when I went to the minors.*

Meanwhile, back at the big gated house on twenty-two acres in Garner, they wondered what to do with me. They went through every emotion—anger, heartbreak, sadness, fear, disgust. They tried to be tough with me, they tried to put their arms around me, they tried everything in between. I was unreachable.

My momma used to say, "We have to live with this every minute of every day, Josh. You have an escape. You get high and forget the problems. We never get a break from it."

My bedroom in the Garner house gave me enough privacy to hide my habit, or at least try. There was a separate entrance and an outdoor storage closet on the patio outside the door.

I kept the paraphernalia for my drug use hidden in my clothes closet. I'd slide the mirror and the razors between a pile of sweatshirts stacked on a shelf so nobody could see them. It was a good hiding spot, and it provided easy access.

I used so much the cocaine tore through my sinuses. I would sit in that room with a T-shirt in my hands, blowing six- to eight-inch-long strings of tissue out of my nose and into the shirt. I could feel them hanging loose behind the bridge of my nose, and I would blow and blow until they came out. The T-shirts were covered in blood and the meaty flesh of my sinuses. I sat there looking at it, happy to have the passage cleared out. I'd take the T-shirt and hide it at the bottom of the closet, or go outside and toss it in the storage closet.

With the evidence hidden and the passages cleared, I'd be good to go. Loose strings of tissue weren't enough to stop me. Blood wasn't enough to stop me. I was unstoppable. With the shirt and the flesh out of the way, I'd get the gear out, open the baggie, and get high. I was adaptable.

■ ■ ■

The doorbell rang in Garner. My parents called me to the front door. When the door opened, there were two DEA agents standing there, flashing their tin. My parents didn't seem surprised.

They came in and sat down. One guy did all the talking.

"Josh, we've been watching you," he said. "We know what you've been doing and where you've been hanging out."

I didn't know what to say, so I said nothing. That seemed to be the only smart choice.

"If we have reason to believe there are drugs in this house, we can come in here and take everything you own," he said. "But we're not interested in you. If we were, we could have gotten you last year."

He then ran down where they had seen me the year before, and what I'd been doing. Four days after I left for spring training in '03, they raided a drug house where I'd spent a lot of time. He was right—they had been watching me.

"We could have had you a bunch of times."

Just because you're paranoid doesn't mean they're not watching you.

They were here now because they were after a dealer in a second-story apartment in Fuquay-Varina. This was an upscale apartment complex near a nice shopping center. The people who lived below the dealer got scared one night when they overheard a conversation through the heating vents. Two people were arguing about getting shorted and getting some stuff that wasn't cocaine. The guy who got shorted started talking about coming back and killing the dealer, so the neighbors called the police and started the process that led to these two men sitting in my living room.

The more they talked, the clearer their motives became. Part of me was relieved that I wasn't going to be leaving the house in handcuffs, but another part of me didn't want to hear what I knew was coming.

"We'd like you to help us," one of them said.

I listened to their proposal. They were trying to get Pete, in order to get someone above him. It was just like in the movies—you help us and we'll agree to leave you alone. They also suggested, with some force, that I change my habits as soon as I finished this operation.

It didn't sound like there was much of a choice to make. I could either cooperate or be arrested. I told them I'd do what I could as long as it didn't threaten my safety.

They didn't need me to change my routine much. I had to keep doing what I was doing, keep going to Pete's house to get drugs, but they wanted me to do it while wearing a wire.

So I did. Twice.

This didn't have the intended effect on me. It should have been a sign that I was so deeply buried in the drug underworld that I was being used by both sides. This development did not cause me to pause and reflect on the wayward course my life had taken. I'm sure many people around me, my parents primarily, allowed a flicker of hope to enter their minds when the DEA agents came to me with their deal.

This would have to provide the wake-up call, right? The scared-straight moment? If he's facing the possibility of arrest and jail time, he's got to seek treatment and make a concerted effort to get better, right?

Wrong. This was no different from every other red flag raised since I began taking drugs. Since I didn't know how to stop, this simply became another no big deal. I could shrug this off, too. Watch me.

■ ■ ■

The treatment centers run together in my mind. I have to think hard to remember the dates and the places and the particulars. There were eight of them, all of the best places in the country—Betty Ford in California, Hazelden in Minnesota, Sierra Tucson, Turning Point in Florida (twice). Expensive, exclusive, and for me, pretty much worthless.

There's a term addicts use for these centers: *spin-dry clinics*. You show up, dry up, and then work to transfer the principles of the twelve-step program to your daily life back in the real world. It works for a lot of people. I wasn't one of them.

The real torment inside me couldn't be addressed in a group setting. I respect the work they do in the clinics, and I have applied many of the teachings to my own sobriety. After all, a reliance on a higher power is the second of the twelve steps, and without Jesus, I would have been dead long ago.

But I got the impression the professionals felt my case was open and shut. Everywhere I went, it was the same: my parents, my parents, my parents. From the first trip to Betty Ford, the story was the same: alone for the first time, free of their shackles, and I lashed out in the worst way possible. They left my side, I left the tracks. Why couldn't I see it?

Well, because I didn't believe it. My parents didn't suffocate me. They didn't keep me from growing up. The professionals kept saying it, but repetition didn't make it fact.

Nearly every counselor carried an expectation that I would agree to blame my parents, and I believe this assumption kept me from dealing with the deeper issues of addiction. They were stubborn, I was stubborn, and the combination took me nowhere.

But think about it from my parents' perspective: They relived every moment that led to my getting involved in drugs. You think they didn't feel responsible? Of course they did. They blamed themselves and wondered what they could have done differently.

I can't count the number of conversations with my mom that started with her saying, "Josh, what did we do wrong to make you want to do this?"

Over and over, I gave her the same response I gave the therapists. "Nothing. You did nothing wrong. I did this myself."

And who knows what would have happened if they hadn't picked up their lives and taken care of me? Maybe it would have happened sooner, or not at all, or exactly the same way. Who knows? Nobody, and that's why it doesn't do anybody any good to assign blame anywhere but with me. It was my life, and my decisions, and I pray every day that I continue to make good ones.

During my first stay at Turning Point, I sat in a group session where everyone discussed their problems and the group chimed in with opinions. One guy, a middle-aged drug dealer/addict who thought he had all the answers, decided to educate me on my problems. He followed the company line and started in on what my parents had done and how it led me to where I was at this moment, sitting in an uncomfortable folding chair listening to him lecture me.

"Your parents were overprotective," he said. "You needed to learn to live on your own."

I started to get angry, and my anger grew the more he spoke. I spoke up for myself, calmly, in an attempt to get him to stop.

"I made the decision to use," I said. "Not my parents."

He kept going, and my anger built. I was not a patient man at this time, but I tried to calm myself by ignoring his words. *This too will pass.* I told myself. Or something like that.

It didn't work. He kept going, as if taunting me. I was the big baseball player with the wasted talent, and he took it upon himself to teach me a lesson. He was going to let me know what I gave up for drugs, as if I didn't already know. I wanted to walk across the circle and tear into him, to beat him till he had no choice but to shut his mouth.

Fortunately, I didn't do that. Instead, I stood up. "I'm done with this," I said. I turned and left the room. I walked to my room and sat on the edge of the bed.

I was furious, and I didn't know what to do with my fury. I wanted to hurt somebody. No, that's not right—I wanted to hurt the guy who had pissed me off. I didn't know what to do with myself. I didn't want to be there, I didn't have anywhere else to go, and I couldn't handle the emotions that were raging through my system.

I lit a cigarette, took a couple of puffs, and then put it on the top of my left hand, with the burning end on the fleshy part between my thumb and index finger. Then I took another cigarette, lit it from the first one, and put it next to it. Then I took another one and did the same. Then another. By the time I was finished I had the burning ends of four cigarettes lined up in a semicircle on the hand that once held the baseball that held my future.

I sat there and looked at it, feeling the heat expand and grow. The flesh began to redden, then sear, my world reduced to this hemisphere of pain. Teeth clenched, I watched. The pain reached a peak and held steady. I could feel it burning through layers, the skin peeling back and curling like newspaper in a fireplace. The smell of my own burning flesh reached my nostrils. I sat transfixed.

The burn grew to about the size of a half-dollar. I took the cigarettes off my hand, one by one, and stubbed them out in an ashtray on the dresser.

I let my body fall backward onto the bed and stared at the ceiling.

I took a deep breath. I felt better, so much better.

■ ■ ■

The drug tests came three times a week, as stipulated in the players' agreement, and in September '03 I blew one off. Failing to take the test is the same as failing the test, so another suspension was in order. Sixty games now. Sixty more games on top of the thirty I'd already missed. Sixty and counting. The next failed test would cost me a full year.

I was lost. Emotionally lost, physically lost, mentally lost. I didn't know where to turn or what to do. Part of my problem, although I didn't know it yet, was denial. I couldn't believe I was using, so I felt I had no choice but to pretend I wasn't.

A positive drug test? I could explain that away. It was a false positive, it was something I ate, it wasn't my pee.

I couldn't believe I was using—that wasn't me, not Josh Hamilton, not the All-American boy—and so I denied I was.

It got to the point where I could convince myself I wasn't using. I operated under a simple principle: If you think it's the truth, then how can it be a lie?

Somehow, I knew enough to know I needed help. I didn't know where to turn, but I knew I had hurt my parents enough to make any meaningful conversation with them impossible at this point.

So I made a decision I still don't know how to explain. I took a drive that ended at the house of Michael Dean Chadwick, the father of my ex-girlfriend Katie. I guess I was looking for advice, or seeking someone who might be able to relate. I remembered how open he was about his bad years, using and selling on the streets of Baltimore. I also remembered how he found sobriety through faith.

It had been close to a year since I'd seen Katie's dad, a man everyone called Big Daddy. I was casting about, and I thought he might be a good place to start.

Big Daddy has a big, beautiful house, and when he answered the door—I arrived unannounced—he greeted me like he had been expecting me all along. Later he told me he had a strange feeling when he opened the door and looked at me. It was eerie, he said, because he opened the door and stared directly into a vision of himself from twenty-five years earlier.

I wasn't real smooth, but I said, "Big Daddy, I was wondering if you had a minute to talk?"

"Of course, Josh," he said. "Come on in. Let's go out back."

We sat on the back patio and talked for at least an hour. I told him I didn't understand what was happening to me, and I wondered if he remembered what it felt like to feel your life slipping away and being powerless to stop it.

He listened to me, and he related segments of his story that were more detailed than anything he'd told me before. His tone was different, and I realized it was a tone that came from experience, from someone who had been in my shoes and knew that BS and lies weren't going to cut it. He was straightforward and unemotional. There was nothing between us, no animosity or disappointment. I hadn't let him down (yet) or hurt his daughter (yet), and he — like many recovering addicts and men of faith — felt it was his responsibility to try to help me through my problems.

Near the end of our conversation, Big Daddy looked at me and shook his head.

"Josh," he said. "There's no magic answer to any of this. I wish there was. But I'll tell you how it works. This will end either one of two ways: You're either going to get better, or you're going to die."

He told me the only way I could get better — truly get better — was through a relationship with Jesus Christ.

His words hung in the air between us. I'd heard variations on the theme since I started using — dead or in jail, that kind of thing — but nobody had put it so bluntly, or delivered the message so dispassionately. Even through my altered vision, the matter-of-fact look in his eyes made an impression on me. He shrugged and gave me a whattaya-gonna-do look.

I appreciated his approach, even if it didn't give me the answers I wanted. I don't even know what answer I wanted. Most people thought they had answers, or knew the right way to scare me back to the right path.

My daddy had a friend who was a sheriff in Wake

County, and once the two of them conspired to scare me straight. They came and picked me up in a squad car and drove me to the jail. They were serious, all business, taking me through the corridor of one of the cell blocks. My daddy's friend had his keys jangling from his belt loop, and he walked up to an empty cell, reached down for his keys, and opened the cell. He ushered me into it. I walked in, kind of amused by the whole process, and then walked out a few minutes later after they realized this exercise wasn't having the desired effect.

They couldn't reach me. Nobody could. I couldn't reach myself, so I had no interest in letting anyone else in. I acted like I had all the answers, even though I had none.

But Big Daddy's words cut through me. Here was someone who'd been through similar times telling me I was going to have to find my way myself.

And where that way took me was entirely up to me.

Before I left he had offered me a job on one of his home-building projects. It was strictly entry-level manual labor, but he thought it would be good for me to feel productive again.

I took the job and spent several weeks digging trenches and doing whatever menial tasks needed to be done. I dealt with Big Daddy standing beside a ditch, looking down at me and saying, "Look at the $4 million man now."

I showed up for work every day, but I was still using and drifting further from where I needed to be. I was still hanging out with Wayne and doing the wrong things. When I told Big Daddy I was going to leave the job, I told him I needed to get out of Raleigh and try to get my mind straight. I had decided to give rehab another shot, this time at Pavillon in the North Carolina hills.

Resigned, I boarded a plane and hoped for the best.

■ ■ ■

How many times had I sat in the television room of a treatment center with my eyes glazed over, ESPN on the screen, my mind somewhere else? More times than anybody could count, probably, and I was doing it again on March 19, 2004, when the news crawl at the bottom of the screen caught my eye: "Devil Rays OF Josh Hamilton suspended for one year for violating MLB drug policy." Those words rolling across the screen informed me that I wouldn't be playing baseball for a while.

Another long while.

This suspension was the big one: number five, one full year. I was the second ballplayer to be punished so severely for violating Major League Baseball's drug policy. The first was Darryl Strawberry. Now he was not alone.

Hazelden in Minnesota was my sixth treatment center. I did well, completing the program and graduating to a halfway house in Tampa run by Turning Point. People who don't understand addiction would see any stay in a program that doesn't result in long-term sobriety as a failure, but I had to look at it differently. I was acquiring tools to deal with the world, a little at a time.

One of the requirements for living in the halfway house was to get a job, and I went down to a big batting cage/baseball school facility and asked for a job. I had to humble myself, by walking in cold off the street to seek employment. The owner was there, and I told him, "I'm living in a halfway house right now, trying to get clean, and I need to get a job as a condition of my living arrangement. I've got a baseball background and I think I can help out around here if you give me a chance."

I never told them my name, and I never tried to use my

baseball status—if it even existed at that time—to get the job. Besides, at that point in my life, I wasn't sure whether my name was going to be a help or a hindrance. Eventually, I could see a flicker of recognition in his eyes, and he asked me my name.

"Josh Hamilton," I said.

He nodded and said, "That's what I thought. I think we can find something to make this work."

I started the next day, cleaning the cages and working with some of the kids who were there for lessons. It was pretty low-level stuff, but I was starting to feel better about myself. For the first time in a while, I could see success in my future.

I stayed clean for four or five months. I felt the urges constantly, and I fought them the way I'd fight off a tough two-strike slider. I tried to keep busy with work and the program. I went to meetings and followed the rules.

Then one day, in a scenario repeated millions of times by millions of addicts, I gave in to a moment of weakness. I left the batting cage one night and stopped at a Wing House restaurant on the way back to the halfway house. I had a few drinks and left, and when I walked back into the facility—late—I was forced to admit to the relapse.

I was probably four miles from resisting temptation and getting back to the halfway house. If I had taken a deep breath and driven straight through, the temptation would have passed.

The pattern is familiar to addicts. You stay clean long enough to see the light, to realize drug use is a hopeless dead end, but then you give in to temptation and ruin everything. The relapse was almost worse than never having stopped, because my hopes would rise and my family would start thinking this was it, I'm finally going to stay clean, and then I'd blow it and everyone would be crest-fallen again.

I didn't have baseball. I was on a revolving suspension plan from Major League Baseball. I felt I couldn't escape, and the feeling of worthlessness stuck to me. The one thing I'd been groomed to do since I was in kindergarten was unavailable to me.

Everywhere I went—"When you gonna get back to playing baseball?"

"Soon, I hope," I said.

I really never believed it.

While I was living in the halfway house and working at the batting cage, I got a visit from Steve Reed, my business manager, and a writer from *ESPN The Magazine.* During that visit, I took batting practice and fielded some balls at a high school field in Tampa, mostly for the magazine's photographer but also for myself. I hadn't been on a field in about eight months, and it felt good. I was shocked by how well I hit the ball and how sharp my reactions were.

No matter what I did to myself, no matter how much I punished my body, the game wouldn't leave it.

I left Turning Point at about the same time the magazine printed the story, which documented my struggle to stay sober but reported how much better I had been doing recently. I left because of that one night I couldn't resist stopping at a Wing House and ordering a few drinks just to see if I could have a couple and stop myself.

I couldn't. The next day I packed up and headed back to Garner. And since I'd already failed, what was the point in staying clean and sober now? In my sick mind, there was none.

ELEVEN

THE PATTERN: Stay clean for a few months, start to feel better, then fall off and be back where I started. I needed a reason to stay clean, even temporarily, and after I'd been home for a month after Turning Point I found one: Katie Chadwick.

We got back together in July 2004, and within four months we decided to get married. It was a big step, obviously, but I was feeling good and being responsible for the first time in a while. I fell head over heels for her daughter, Julia, and the two of them made me happy without drugs and alcohol.

While Katie and I were together, I stayed clean. I went to AA meetings nearly every day. My sobriety and my actions led her to believe my days of using were over. I believed it, too. Because of my suspension, baseball remained on the margins of my life, more in thought than in action.

I thought Katie wanted a big church wedding, but every time we agreed on a date someone had a problem with it. Finally, Katie said, "I don't really care how we do it, I just want to be your wife." I said, "Great, let's get married tomorrow."

So we did. We were married at the Raleigh courthouse

on November 10, 2004, before an audience of my parents, Katie's parents, and a few others. For a honeymoon, we spent a couple nights at a bed-and-breakfast outside Raleigh. I was tied to the AA meetings, so we decided on a short honeymoon that didn't take us very far away.

In December, Katie got pregnant.

Everything moved fast, faster than I expected.

We bought a house in the town of Fuquay-Varina, a few miles from where I grew up. It was a big house in a cul-de-sac, with a large lot. It was less than a quarter-mile from a nice fishing pond, and we were happy to start a new life together. I still considered myself a ballplayer, and I started to believe I could wait out the suspension and get back in the game.

Katie had never seen me play baseball in high school, and since we reconnected I had been either injured or suspended. To her, I wasn't really a ballplayer, and I might never be again. That didn't matter to her; she was willing to accept me with all my problems attached.

But at this time, other than not really having a job, I didn't have that many problems. I was clean, I was married, I was relatively happy. Then, in January, less than a month after we learned Katie was pregnant, I relapsed. I traveled the well-worn track of my addiction: first too many drinks in a bar, then some coke, then back to the bar.

In my experience, it's common for an addict to slip up and then set off on a major binge. The guilt of relapsing takes over and you figure what's the use? But this time, I got myself back together, shrugged it off as a one-time thing, and got back to my life.

For four months, I stayed clean. Then, on my twenty-fourth birthday—Saturday, May 21, 2005—I brought a bottle of Crown Royal with me to an afternoon birthday party at Katie's parents' house. After the party, the plan was for Katie, Julia, and me to meet my parents for dinner at a local restaurant. Over and over, I left the party for a few minutes to sneak to the truck. I would then re-emerge, drunker each time. There was a cake, and one of Katie's first hints that I was messed up came when she watched me fumble and stumble as I tried to cut the cake. I had been so good for so long she was completely shocked this was happening.

We had to leave to meet my parents for dinner. By the time we got into Katie's Toyota Sequoia, a Christmas present from me, I was slurring my words and becoming nastier by the minute. I sat in the passenger's seat, reeling.

"You're embarrassing me," Katie said as we drove off. "I can't believe you're doing this."

The conversation deteriorated from there. I could be a nasty, mean drunk, and I flew into a white-hot rage. I punched the windshield so hard it cracked. I demanded she let me out. Disgusted with me and upset that Julia was witnessing such a display, she pulled over on the highway.

I took off directly into the woods along the shoulder of the road. I didn't have a destination in mind, but I wanted to be as far away as possible from everybody. I was turning twenty-four, and I should have been seven weeks into my second or third big-league season. Instead I was stumbling through the pine trees along Highway 64 outside Cary, North Carolina.

Katie drove back to her parents' house, furious and sad at the same time. She told them what happened and Big Daddy and a friend of his decided to drive around and look for me. They found me, at a gas station a few miles from where Katie let me out. They brought me back to Big Daddy's house.

It didn't get any better. I felt trapped, and my anger spiked again when I got back to the house. It reached a peak when I stood at the end of the long driveway that snakes toward the pool in the back of this beautiful house in this beautiful neighborhood and challenged Big Daddy and his friend.

I pulled a baseball bat out of the cab of my truck and snapped it over my knee. I tossed one half to Big Daddy and the other to his friend. Then I shouted, "You're going to need those if you plan on coming after me."

I had incredible strength when my mind was altered. I once picked up my daddy and moved him away from the doorway in our Garner house because he tried to stand between me and the door. My father is a large man, thick and strong, and yet I moved him the way I would a kitchen chair.

On this night, I felt the strength and rage coiled inside me. I was trapped by addiction, and by my inability to do the right thing. After I broke the bat and challenged them, they told me to leave or they would call the cops. I responded by slamming my fist against one of the sideview mirrors of their friend's truck.

Justifiably fearing what I might do next, they called the police. Two cops showed up at the house and I went with them without much fuss. They took me to the station and put me in the drunk tank to sober up. Disgusted and angry, I sat there silently and slept little. I had blown four months of sobriety — and blown them big-time — and my reaction was to stay pissed off at the people around me and pretend the drinking was no big deal. I didn't use, I just drank — what was so bad about that? The next morning, a Sunday, they called me out of the tank and sent me on my way with no charges filed.

Instead of calling Katie to pick me up, I took my

belongings, headed out the door, and started walking. The police shrugged and gave me a suit-yourself look when I told them I wasn't calling anyone for a ride. I decided to head for my grandma's house, to the one place I could always go to relax and avoid judgment. She'd open the door, no questions asked.

It was a ten-mile walk, but I didn't care.

I was in no hurry.

■ ■ ■

Back on the hamster wheel, back to disappointment and resentment, back to square one. I'd go a week or two without using, then I'd use, then I'd go a week or two or maybe even three without using again.

For the first time, money became an issue. Drugs and repeated trips to rehab had cost me somewhere in the neighborhood of $500,000. When Katie and I got back together, I had about $500,000 left over from my signing bonus, and we put about $100,000 of that down on the new house. My erratic behavior had made Katie leery of giving me free rein on the bank accounts, so we started a game of keep-away with money. She would move it, and I would try to find it. The $3.96 million signing bonus—with nearly half going to taxes—wouldn't last forever.

But I wasn't the type of addict to let something as insignificant as insufficient funds—or reduced access—get in the way of my drug use. Again, I adapted. In August, with Katie pregnant, I needed some coke but had no means of buying it.

Katie had stopped wearing her wedding ring—we weren't officially separated, but it was heading that way. She was pregnant, and we weren't spending much time together. I went into the house when she wasn't home and got her wedding ring out of the bedroom. I drove to a dealer's house and told him he could keep the ring as collateral until I got my hands on some money.

He was fine with that, and I left the ring and got what I needed. I had been reduced to this: pawning my wife's wedding ring for drugs.

The next day, when Katie discovered the ring missing, she was livid. She not only let me have it, but she tracked down the dealer's number and arranged to meet with him in a parking lot to get the ring back.

"I understand you have my wedding ring," she said on the phone.

After the guy said something smart, Katie said, "You're going to give it back. You have no right to that."

The dealer agreed, providing he got some money in return, and my pregnant wife drove to a parking lot, met with this character, and made the exchange. She had never been so scared in her life, but no matter what she thought about me at the time, she wasn't about to let my lifestyle destroy all the dignity in our life.

■　■　■

Sierra Hamilton was born on August 22, 2005.

I was there with Katie at the hospital. I had three really good days after Sierra was born.

And on the fourth day, Katie sent me out to the drugstore to pick up a prescription for her. Instead of going to the drugstore, I went to a bar.

I didn't want to be good anymore. I couldn't handle the pressure or the responsibility or the feeling of being fenced in by a family and a life I wasn't sure I deserved.

I drank, I used. I took off on a wild ride that would have killed most people.

I became impossible to live with. I would leave to get a can of dip and not come back for three days. Katie would call and call and get the same answer: "This is Josh, leave a message." How many times did she call me, with a new-born and a four-and-a-half-year-old to care for, hoping just to hear my voice, to know that I was still alive, only to get that recording?

Most of the time, I would set out to do what I intended to do: buy a can of dip. But then I'd see a bar or get a craving. Once that happened, nothing else mattered. I could walk into a bar, order a Crown Royal, and be done with the real world for the better part of a week. In my mind, I didn't have anywhere to be, no job or obligations, so who really cared how I spent my days?

The pattern was strikingly similar. I would begin to drink, then I'd start to get drunk, then I'd want some coke so I could keep drinking and stay up and do whatever I felt like doing. Restaurants and bars, in my experience, are rats' nests of drugs. I could sit at the bar, minding my own business, and within no time I could identify the people working there who would be able to get me drugs or know who might. It was like picking up the spin of a curveball in the millisecond after it leaves the pitcher's hand.

Sometimes, Katie couldn't take not knowing where I was. I was sitting at a bar in Cary, hanging out with a group of people, when Katie walked in and strolled right up to the bar.

I noticed her feet—she wasn't wearing shoes. She was so frustrated with calling me and not getting an answer that she got in the car and went searching. She didn't bother to wear shoes, probably because she had no real hope of finding her vagabond husband. So when she saw my truck in front of the restaurant, not that far from our home, she was so pissed she got out and came in to get me.

And even though she might have wanted to haul me out of there by my ear, she didn't. Maybe she knew that was a hopeless cause.

She just never understood why I would prefer this life. I had a wife and two little girls at home, including a beautiful newborn. I had a wife who loved me despite everything. I had a support structure of my parents and in-laws and my brother and my grandma. I had a life out there, a good life, and Katie couldn't understand why I turned my back on it to live a life of random encounters with strangers who shared nothing more than a desire to get high.

I didn't understand it, either. I just did it. I never gave much thought to it. It controlled my life. Everything I did seemed to revolve around it—wanting it, getting it, using it, wanting it all over again. It's a cliché to call it a vicious circle, but that's exactly what it is. The drug's greatest power is to make you want more. As soon as you get it, you start thinking about getting more. It's the hamster wheel of drug abuse: You keep running, you get nowhere.

I stopped claiming I was going to clean up. I stopped pretending, I guess, and I stopped saying things because I thought people would get off my back if I could convince them I was willing to try one more time.

One day I was sitting alone in our house in Fuquay-Varina, just sitting in the front room watching television, when I heard something out front. When I looked out through the living-room window I saw a SWAT team assembling in the street. They were all suited up in their riot gear, and they were preparing for an assault on my house.

I panicked. I had an eight ball (an eighth of an ounce) of cocaine in the house, and I was sure they were preparing to bust my door down to come and get it. I ran to where I had it stashed and proceeded to sit down and inhale it. All of it. In a matter of seconds.

This was enough coke to kill some people. It was insanity, a death wish, like pulling out my heart and smacking it with a two-by-four.

Most people, even hard-core users, would have flushed the stuff down the toilet and been done with it. Not me. I couldn't waste it, so I used it.

My heart starting pounding in my chest, faster and faster, till I could see it bouncing through my shirt.

The doorbell rang. It was somebody selling something.

■　■　■

It's painful to recall these memories. I'm not proud of any of them, but I'm confident someone can learn from them. I'm confident there's a higher purpose, that everything happened so I can be here now, sharing my story. I need to turn this pain to joy.

I made several trips to the emergency room. Sometimes I took myself, sometimes other people took me there and dropped me off. If I hadn't been so young and strong, I doubt I would have made it. I stressed my heart so many times I don't know what lies ahead, but I try not to think about that.

The mornings were the worst. I would wake up, or still be awake, after a night of heavy using. I would feel my heart beating in my chest and swear it wasn't working right. It was too fast, or irregular, or pounding so hard it might spring through my rib cage. I would fixate on it, feeling it and watching it and believing I could hear it.

Every time, I was sure I was going to die. I was completely sure, no questions asked, so I would drive in a state of panic to the hospital and walk into the emergency room.

I never consciously tried to kill myself, but there were many times when I ingested enough cocaine to accidentally overdose. It's only by the grace of God and my big strong body that I didn't end up dead.

These trips to the emergency room all happened before Katie and I got married, and each time my parents were forced to come to the hospital. Worn down by the constant worry, they were left to hope that I would reach bottom and be forced to get clean. They had lost faith in the treatment centers and scare tactics and tough love that had failed over and over.

I very nearly overdosed and found myself in the ER during one period of binge usage. My mom came into the room and stood next to the bed. She had long since lost her patience for my behavior, and my shame was clear. I pretended not to care what anybody said or thought, but I was in anguish. I could tell by the look on her face how bad I must have looked, and how badly it hurt her to sit there and look at me. There were tears in her eyes. I wanted to stop, but I couldn't promise anything. I didn't know where to start.

She sat there for quite some time in a thick silence. I had nothing to say, and an apology seemed inadequate at this stage of my deterioration.

In a voice barely above a whisper, she said something I couldn't quite hear.

"What was that, Momma?" I asked.

Just a little bit louder, with her head shaking and her voice breaking, she said, "God must love ballplayers."

I didn't understand. I hadn't played baseball for more than two years, and I wasn't even sure I was a baseball player anymore. Normally, I ignored or shrugged off everything someone said to me, especially if I thought it was just more browbeating intending to make me stop using drugs.

But this confused me, and made me curious. Why was she bringing up baseball?

"What are you talking about, Momma?"

"It's simple, Josh," she said. "If God didn't love ball-players, you'd have been dead a long time ago."

■ ■ ■

Katie was on her own. She didn't know what happened to me, or whether this was temporary or permanent. This was supposed to be the happiest moment of our lives — bringing our beautiful newborn home to our house — and here was Katie, all by herself wondering where the hell I was and what I was doing. She lived in a world where she could send her husband to the drugstore for a prescription and end up with neither the medicine nor a husband.

I missed Katie, I missed Julia, and I missed Sierra. It didn't matter, though, because the tidal pull of drugs was so much stronger than any guilt or responsibility I might have felt toward them.

Justifiably, Katie wondered whether I would ever make it home again.

One night about three weeks after Sierra was born, I befriended a guy and his girlfriend at a bar. I was craving some coke so I could keep drinking, and I identified them as likely suspects.

When I asked them if they knew where I could get

some, they did me one better: They said they knew where we could score some crack.

By this time, I wasn't particular about my drug use. I couldn't stomach downers—I never tried heroin, marijuana made me vomit—but if it was a stimulant, I was good with it. These two were telling me my life would never be the same after crack, the high was so much better than powder—okay, I said, I'm up for it. They didn't need the hard sell.

We drove away from town, down a narrow, dark, two-lane road that ribbons its way into the country past small ranches and ragged trailer parks. We made a left into the entrance of one of those dilapidated trailer parks.

Four years before, I would have punched the gas pedal to get past a place like this as soon as possible. Now I was getting out of the car and walking up a wobbly wooden staircase to get inside. We were met by three black men. I would guess they were in their mid-thirties, but it's tough to determine the age of a crack addict. They were abnormally thin and their skin was bad, which made them look older. Dental hygiene was not an obsession. The trailer was dirty and hot, and the guys—they were introduced to me as Murd, Leon, and Lester—struck me as kind of scary.

No matter. They had something we wanted. We paid for the stuff and sat down to get started. I didn't know much about crack, but I learned. You can either poke a hole in a Coke can and smoke it through that, or you can stop at a convenience store and purchase one of those fake roses in the plastic bud vase they keep near the register. These are not intended for guys to impress their girls; they're cheap and easy crack pipes.

For the price of a ninety-nine-cent rosebud and a box of Chore Boy scouring pads, you can be in business. Pop off the removable cap at the bottom of the rosebud, pack it with Chore Boy, and burn it till all that's left of the Chore Boy is the copper wire.

The copper wire serves to hold the rock in place and as a filter to allow the smoke to go through. I watched as they went through this process, then took the pipe and—once again—changed my life.

From the moment the drug hit my brain I was hit with a rush of euphoria that could never be replicated.

It was a feeling I'd want, again and again.

I proved it over the next six weeks, when I burned through about $100,000 on drugs. Crack was my new best friend.

Money accelerated from a concern to an obsession. Katie was trying to keep our household going with no income and an erratic and uncontrollable outflow from my drug use. As if she didn't have enough on her mind, she had a new household task: keep me away from the rest of our money.

Something changed inside Katie when she found I was using crack. Cocaine seemed controllable, treatable, maybe even understandable. But crack? Crack was lowlife, dead end. You did crack when you didn't care anymore. The crackhead occupied society's basement. You did crack as a sign to the world that you'd given up.

I dove in headfirst. I smoked crack like it could save the world. From the moment the high wore off, I was searching for it again. The low was indescribable. I woke up in the cab of my pickup, or in places I didn't recognize with people I didn't know, and I'd pray to the Lord to take me away from the nightmare my life had become.

I prayed to be spared another day of the guilt and depression and addiction. I prayed I would spare the people I loved further disappointment. I prayed to be taken away.

My descent to the bottom accelerated in a manner that shocked and frightened even the people who had watched me self-destruct for the previous three years.

And still I used. I was caught in a horrible downward spiral, and I couldn't pull out. The brief euphoria can't be replicated, but the hideousness of the drug makes you try and try till you either die or somehow give it up.

I didn't care about anything else. I stopped eating, and the weight dropped off me like I was throwing it out the window of my pickup. I could lose fifteen pounds a week, just by living for crack. There were days I forgot to eat.

My relationship with Katie disintegrated, and yet one day she looked me in the eye and said, "God spoke to my soul and told me someday you're going to be back playing baseball. Josh, there's a bigger plan for you. When you come back, it's going to be about more than baseball."

Katie was not a baseball person. She was not with me because of baseball. The game was never more than a shadow in our relationship.

I couldn't look her in the eye. There was something about the way she was talking, something about the intensity of her words and manner, that made me look away.

"Yeah, yeah, quit talking to me," I said.

"Okay, but just remember what I said."

■ ■ ■

Here's a funny story: After my freshman year in high school, I played on an American Legion summer baseball team, and one week we took a trip to Johnson County, in the heart of the North Carolina tobacco country.

It was midsummer, and the weather was unbearable. It was something like ninety-eight degrees with a 98 percent humidity. The tobacco fields began just a few feet beyond the outfield fence and kept going as far as you could see. Behind the left-field fence there was a tobacco processing plant.

I played right field, and the smell coming off the tobacco plants started to make me feel queasy about the second inning. With the heat and the humidity, the leaves gave off an odor that made me feel as if those leaves were packed in my nostrils.

In the stands, my parents looked out at me and wondered what was wrong. I was doubled over, with a pained look on my face, like I was about to throw up. I couldn't wait for every inning to end so I could get back to the dugout and away from the smell as fast as possible.

Why is this a funny story? Because I think back to that day and wonder how I could go from being a kid who couldn't stand the smell of tobacco leaves to a man who would sit in a trailer with a bunch of lowlife strangers and inhale crack into his lungs for a cheap high.

■ ■ ■

My money woes didn't let up. None was coming in, and a lot was going out. My business managers, Steve Reed and Ken Gamble, still had access to my bank accounts. When one account ran dry, they could move money into another and allow me to access it through an ATM card or checks. I started to call them for money, over and over.

"Ken, can I get $300 moved over?"

"Hey Steve, I need about $200. Can you make it happen?"

It became an obsession. I would call them at their offices in California over and over. I would be driving around, waiting to get some product, and if the call went to voicemail I'd end the call and call back immediately. I repeated this as long as it took for me to get hold of one of them. I wouldn't take no for an answer.

Steve and Ken knew my problems, and they kept in touch long after I stopped being an asset to them. When I received my signing bonus, they set me up as a corporation, with my parents as partners. This turned out to be prescient, in ways nobody could have predicted at the time.

When my drug use veered out of control, Steve called my daddy and told him the time had come for him to invoke power of attorney through the corporation. There was no brake pedal in my life; it was all accelerator, all the time, and I was going to keep flooring it until there was nothing left of me or my bank account. This way, by invoking power of attorney, my parents could take control of my money and keep me from bankrupting myself.

Despite all the problems and heartbreak I had caused, I think deep down my daddy still had hopes I would get better. He couldn't allow himself to believe otherwise, and the idea of wresting control of my finances carried a sense of finality—of surrender—that he tried hard to avoid. What Steve presented was a realistic view of where my life stood, though, and what could happen in the future. It was difficult for my daddy to absorb.

After the proposal was laid out to him, my daddy thought for a moment and said, "Boy, Steve, I don't know if I want to do that to him."

"I know you don't," Steve said. "Nobody does, but your son's going to kill himself the way he's headed. You need to do what you can to stop him. He's going to end up giving every last cent to drug dealers."

Steve convinced my daddy it was the right thing to do, and he eventually did it. I don't think I even knew it happened, but now I'm glad it did. We were at least able to salvage something, which was important. At that stage of the game, I wouldn't have stopped till it was all gone.

I'd do anything to get the money to get drugs. Katie came home once to find me unscrewing the television set from the wall. I was going to barter it for crack. In the same way I pawned Katie's wedding ring for drugs, I used my New York–Penn League championship ring from 1999, my first year in pro baseball, to get crack. I gave one of the guys from the trailer the ring to hold till I got money (same old story), and this time I never did. He kept the ring, and I never pursued it. It's out there somewhere, the only championship ring I ever won, another casualty of my addiction.

I was feral, free of rules, unconcerned with anyone else's feelings. I wrote a check for $2,000 to Murd, assuring him the check was good and actually believing it. This was traditionally a cash business, but he agreed to take a check. I was out of options. By the time he tried to cash it, the account was closed. Katie, in an attempt to save what was left of our dwindling resources, moved the money into another account and didn't allow me access.

I was furious. My mind was so messed up I felt this was my money and I could spend it any way I wanted. My self-absorption and selfishness didn't leave room for me to see how it would affect other people. It was about me, and about drugs, and nothing else mattered.

I figured I could work on Katie to get some money in the account, enough to cover it. As soon as the guy found out the check bounced, he'd come after me. It wouldn't be pretty. These were not guys you tried to screw over.

I explained, and Katie said no. I begged, and still she said no.

I tried to scare her, to tell her what might happen to me, to her, to the kids.

She stood firm.

The guy began to call. He threatened me, and gave me a deadline. Just like the movies. I had forty-eight hours.

Katie was scared, but she wouldn't budge. She did, however, tell her father about my predicament.

Big Daddy called me and said, "Josh, give me his name and phone number, and I'll take care of it."

"No," I said. "I don't want you involved in this. I have the money. I just need Katie to let me have it."

Big Daddy can be pretty forceful when he needs to be. He told me no matter what I said, he was not going to allow Katie to release that money.

I still disagreed, but I had no choice but to give in. I didn't want anyone else in my business, but he was solving a problem for me.

Big Daddy called the guy to set up a meeting to hand over the cash.

"Will you be packing?"

"Do I need to be?" Big Daddy answered.

That was all Big Daddy needed to know. If they're asking, the answer is yes, you need to pack.

They set up a meeting in the parking lot of a shopping mall. Both of them were packing when they got out of the car, and before Big Daddy handed the cash to Murd he said, "Let's get something straight. I'm paying you this one time, but if you ever try to sell Josh drugs again, I'm coming after you."

The guys laughed. Who *was* this crazy SOB? But while they laughed, Big Daddy never took his eyes off them.

"Listen to me," he said. "I've been where you guys are. I'm a little bit crazy, and I'm not afraid to die. So you have to decide if you want to take the chance."

They stopped laughing. The look in their eyes was a little bit different. They took the money and nodded.

"Now, I'm not kidding," Big Daddy said. "Remember that."

Big Daddy got into his Escalade and drove off. With the adrenaline still rushing, and the moment still inside him, he was startled by the ring of his phone. He expected it to be his wife, Janice, or maybe Katie—someone wanting to know how it went down.

He answered. It was Murd.

"Hey, you want to come to work for me?"

■ ■ ■

Katie talked to me about disappointment and loss. Her parents talked to me about disappointment and loss. Everybody talked to me about disappointment and loss.

Mostly, my parents spoke to me about disappointment and loss. They were frustrated, and they told me about how many people I had let down and how much pain I had caused.

My daddy called me outside one day at our house in Garner. He wanted to take a walk. We walked around the pond below the house, not saying much, the shambles of my life caught in the silence.

Finally, Daddy said, "Josh, you know it hurts me to see you waste away before my eyes, don't you?"

I nodded, steeling myself for another in a long line of lectures that I had no interest in hearing.

"You know it hurts your mother, too, don't you?"

I nodded.

"It hurts us to see you ruin your life, and we can't do anything about it."

"It hurts me, too," I said. "It hurts me more."

This caught him off-guard. He didn't expect this answer. I had always shrugged off whatever he had to say and then gone on and done whatever I wanted anyway. My parents took that as a sign that I didn't care what they had to say, and that I wasn't at all bothered by what had become of my life.

I could sense my daddy tense up. His frustration was boiling over into anger.

Through clenched teeth, he said, "If it hurts you, then why don't you just stop it?"

I had no answer. I shrugged and looked away. No addict, in the middle of the addiction, has any hope of answering that question. He didn't understand it, and I didn't understand it. We had reached the addict's impasse. He was out of solutions. I was out of answers.

But that's the question, right? *Why don't you just stop it?* That's the central question asked of every addict by every person who loves him. It's the question you would have asked, and the question I would have asked if the roles had been reversed.

If you know you're hurting people, and you can see it, and you know what's causing it, why don't you just stop?

If only it were that easy.

If only.

TWELVE

I WAS DISINTEGRATING; there was no getting around it. My life narrowed to the pursuit and use of drugs. Everything else was secondary. I didn't have the interest, or the time, for anything else. Make no mistake, there was no joy in this life. I was miserable — paranoid, sick, unable to think straight. I cared about nobody, especially not myself. I couldn't remember the last time I laughed or even smiled or felt a flutter of joy pass through me. I was living like an animal.

On a typically messed-up day in the late summer of '05, when crack ruled my life, I was sitting at the bar in Chili's when I met up with a group of guys who had graduated from Athens Drive High a few years before me. They weren't my friends, and they were barely acquaintances. If I had passed these guys on the street five years before, I would have nodded in recognition without ever dreaming I'd be part of their group. And now we were sitting in a bar, hanging out like best buds. The rules had changed.

I'd been smoking on and off that day. As always, I was chasing the high to keep from facing the low. When we'd had enough of the bar, we went to a house where one of the guys lived. I drove my truck, even though I had no business being behind the wheel.

When we got there, I smoked more and drank more. One of the guys had some pills, and he told me he had something I needed to try. At this point, I had crossed every threshold, so why not?

He handed me half a Klonopin. I'd never taken this before, but of course I dropped it in my mouth without asking any questions. Klonopin is a drug in the same family as Valium and Xanax. It's a sedative used as an anti-seizure medication for panic disorders, and it's also used as an amnesic to provide conscious sedation. It can result in blackouts and partial memory loss.

But since Klonopin works to stop rapid heartbeat and unexplained sweating, it's something crack addicts use to offset the effects of the drug. When you become immersed in the drug culture, you learn all the tricks. I was a user rather than a student of drug use, but I learned that using one drug against another is a true measure of sickness. Of course, when you're the one who is sick you're not thinking that way. Or thinking much at all.

The combination of alcohol, crack, and Klonopin sent me reeling. Klonopin is a downer, and I've always had severe reactions to downers. My vision got blurry, and everything around me slowed. I no longer felt social. Eventually I blacked out, but I didn't have the good fortune of passing out. I was in the fog-world of the consciously sedated.

I don't remember anything that happened in the next five or six hours. At some point, I left the so-called party and drove my Chevy pickup to visit Katie's parents at their house. Again, based on what I've been told, I was shouting and carrying on in front of the house. As I was leaving

I stumbled and fell, hitting my head on an air compressor near the garage. They had visitors, so I don't think my presence was appreciated.

Next I drove to the house in Fuquay-Varina, where Katie and the girls were sleeping. I was a frightening sight, all glassy-eyed and incoherent. She tried to get me to stop driving around, but she didn't want to let me in because she was afraid and didn't want the girls to see me in this condition. She went back into the house and prayed through her tears.

I left. Apparently I decided to head for the trailer park, where I could get more crack. I had a one-track mind, and I didn't even need to be conscious to want more. Over time, users build up a resistance to crack and reach the point where they need more and more to recapture the feeling of the first high. In the vicious cycle of drug abuse, crack is the endgame. It eats you up from the inside out.

I got back into the truck and headed out for the twenty-minute drive from my house in Fuquay-Varina to the crack house. The road is a two-lane country highway, narrow with almost no shoulder, flanked by pine forests and farmlands.

It was late, after midnight, and I was consumed with the idea of getting to my guys Murd and Lester and Leon. I guess I had a few bucks in my pocket, enough to get a couple of rocks that would get me through what was left of the night.

At some unknown point along the highway, my truck ran out of gas. I got out and left it, so consumed by my mission that walking must have struck me as a sane option.

So I walked. And walked. Up and down the hilly terrain and along the extended stretches of straightaway through landscape alternating between pine forests and farmlands. Every so often a nice new McMansion sits alongside the road, not far from a trailer park or a run-down farmhouse.

This is country, which means the stars and the moon serve as street lights. Traffic is not a big concern. The cicadas and crickets were chirping, and my T-shirt was soaked in sweat on the hot night.

I don't know how long I'd been walking when I suddenly emerged from the fog and became aware of my own existence. It was like surfacing after being underwater. I had long since lost the ability to surprise myself with my powers of self-destruction, but what I saw when the blackout lifted took me a moment to comprehend.

Between my feet I saw the double-yellow center stripe in the middle of the road. Ahead of me about one hundred yards I saw a pair of headlights, moving in my direction.

I was walking down the center of the highway, oblivious. What a sad sight I must have been: disheveled, wobbly, haggard, covered in tattoos advertising who I once was, walking miles away from my abandoned truck in a quest for more crack.

I was a shell of a human, a soulless being. I had stripped myself of self-respect and lost my ability to feel love or hope or joy or even pain. After I awoke, after I became aware that I was walking down the middle of a narrow, pitch-black, two-lane highway with headlights approaching, I didn't change anything.

I stayed where I was, right down the middle of the road.

■ ■ ■

A car came up from behind, slowing to a crawl, inching next to me. The driver was a Mexican man in his early

forties. The look on his face expressed a mixture of concern and fear, as if he wasn't sure he should be stopping but
couldn't live with himself if he didn't.

Tentatively, he asked, "Do you need some help?"

Buddy, I thought, you don't want to go there.

"I guess I ran out of gas," I said. "I need a ride up the
road."

I was hot and sweating, and I'm sure I was a hell of
a sight. I'm sure there was a crazed look on my face—a
look you might associate with a guy who would walk for
miles in the dead of night to get crack. He thought for a
moment, probably assessing his chances to survive the trip,
and then told me to get in. We started up the highway,
winding our way through the darkness. He dropped me
off in front of the trailer park. I thanked him and stumbled
down the gravel road past a row of trailers that popped up
like mushrooms amid the pines. My good Samaritan sped
off quickly.

Murd and Leon were awake, of course—that's one
thing about crackheads, you usually don't have to worry
about waking them up late at night. They liked to see me
coming, because they remembered the days when I paid
for more product than I got. Those were my days of high
liquidity, and those days were permanently in the past.

During the summer of '05, I flew through $100,000 on
crack and other drugs. Even the false glamour of snorting
coke during a night at a club had long since passed me by.
I was a freebaser, a crack addict. I knew all the tricks; I
bought the rosebuds and the Chore Boys at the gas-station
stores and tossed the fake roses out the truck window as
soon as I hit the road. I burned the copper off the Chore
Boy to create the filter that allowed me to smoke through
the rosebud while the Chore Boy wire held the rock in

place. I would pull that corrosive smoke into my lungs and feel a brief wave of euphoria.

And during my time with the guys in the trailer I picked up another handy skill: One night Murd got out the baking soda (one part) and the coke (two parts) and taught me how to cook cocaine into rock form.

The night of the blackout, I passed out on the dirty floor of the trailer. I had stopped caring, or maybe I stopped being able to care, and spending the night in this unsavory place with these sketchy characters was yet another example. I was rapidly losing touch with who I used to be. The athlete, the son, the husband—I had to think hard to remember who that guy was. The photos at my parents' house of me in my various uniforms might as well have been old family photos of a deceased relative.

I prayed to God to take me away, to release me from this hellish life. I couldn't escape on my own. Death was the only possible relief.

I woke up that morning in an empty trailer. The heat was stifling. It was so hot and humid inside that metal trailer that I felt like I had been wrapped in aluminum foil and placed in an oven. I pulled myself to my feet and went outside. I felt terrible. My truck was parked in front of the trailer. Someone went out and got my truck during the night, which wasn't that surprising. When I started running low on available cash, I used my truck to barter for drugs. I'd let them make their runs in my truck in exchange for drugs. Hey, whatever it takes. As I climbed in that morning, I noticed the quarter-panel on the driver's side was bashed in.

Did I do that, or did they? Either was possible. I didn't ask, and I never found out. It just didn't seem that important at the time.

THIRTEEN

GRANNY WAS AWAKE when my truck rumbled up her driveway at 2:15 A.M. I parked and staggered up the walk to the wooden door at the front of the screened-in porch in the house fifty yards from where I grew up. I was weak, strung out, emaciated. I was coming down from another major crack binge with Murd, Lester, Leon, and a couple of other guys I barely knew in the dirty trailer outside town. I couldn't remember the last time I had slept. My clothes hung off me, the emptiness a pathetic reminder of who I used to be. My once-strong body was reduced to 180 pounds. I was a waste.

Before I arrived at Granny's, I left the trailer and started driving...where? Home? Hardly. Katie got a restraining order against me so she could sell the house in Fuquay-Varina without worrying about me showing up in God-knows-what condition. My parents didn't want me, and who could blame them, either? There weren't many doors that would open for me.

Drugs had destroyed my body and my mind and my spirit. I could no longer experience happiness or surprise. I couldn't remember the last time I felt spontaneous joy. Why was I even alive?

Why was I still here? Why was my life spared?

Was it because, as my momma suggested, God loves baseball players?

Or was it because, as Katie swore, God had bigger plans for me?

It was October 1, 2005. The Major League Baseball pennant races were in final stage, a fact that couldn't have been further from my mind. I was no longer a baseball player; I was a crack addict, a junkie.

Granny didn't know I was coming. She hadn't seen me in two or three months. It was two in the morning. I had no money, no place to stay, and no plan for any of it. I was reverting to the actions of my childhood, when Granny's house served as my haven, a refuge when I needed to feel comfortable and wanted. I wasn't thinking straight, but somewhere inside me I knew I would be welcome at Granny's, and that I didn't have to worry about being judged.

I was a wreck—dirty, twitchy, barely coherent. I was so absorbed in my own world I didn't consider the circumstances of my presence here. I didn't think about the rudeness of showing up at the doorstep of a seventy-two-year-old woman in the middle of the night. This house afforded me the best chance of finding temporary shelter, so here I was. Here's how my mind worked: If Granny let me in, and I knew she would, I could stay here for a day or two until I could figure out where I could find some money and get back to scoring drugs.

Granny met me at the door in her robe. She must have heard me rumbling into the driveway, or else she was already awake. I didn't have the wherewithal to ask.

She opened the door and said, simply, "Josh."

She hid the shock she must have felt at the sight of me.

There was food on my T-shirt, I was fidgety and sweating, I couldn't stand still. My nose was congested, causing me to sniffle constantly. There was blood caked on the outside of my nostrils. I had a nasty cough.

"Hi, Granny. Do you think I can stay here for a little while?"

"You don't look too good, Josh. How about you come in and get you something to eat?"

Once I got into the house, Granny suggested I take a shower while she cooked me some eggs. There was no doubt I needed to clean up. When I got out, she had a plate of eggs waiting for me. She was in the spare bedroom fixing up the bed.

Shame began to creep into my thoughts. What was I doing? What was I putting her through? But I was desperate, too, and the desperation overrode the shame. I needed to be somewhere, and this was the last refuge. I sat down at the small table in Granny's kitchen and silently ate the eggs while Granny watched.

I was unsteady and unsure of myself. Even the smallest actions were a chore. When I finished eating, Granny told me to come to bed. She led me to the bedroom and stood beside the bed, pulling down the bedcovers. Like a child following orders, I lay down. Granny pulled the covers up to my chin and leaned over. She kissed me on the forehead without saying a word.

I hadn't been in a bed for days, maybe a week. Granny turned out the light and closed the door. She walked across the TV room to her bedroom, where she dropped onto the bed and began crying, softly at first, before deep sobs overtook her. She lay awake with her tears until exhaustion carried her off to sleep.

■ ■ ■

The next morning, Granny went to work. She woke me up at ten-thirty and put me in front of another large plate of eggs. "You're going to eat, Josh," she said. "You've got to gain your strength back."

My idea—to use Granny's house as a temporary shelter on my way back to using—wasn't her idea. If I was going to show up and ask for help, she was going to give it. She sat down next to me at the kitchen table and told me she wasn't going to let me sleep all day because I needed to get up and get food in me if I was going to start feeling better.

My brother Jason and his family lived in our old family home next door to Granny, so it didn't take long for everyone to learn that I had shown up on Granny's doorstep, and that she had opened her door to me and taken me in. The reaction was immediate. Everyone in the family told her she was making a mistake, that I should be left to my own devices if I insisted on living the life of an addict.

Granny disagreed. She is a headstrong southern lady, and all the warnings—that she was enabling me, that I needed to hit bottom—gave her more reason to dig in her heels and prove to everybody that she knew better. She could cure me, she thought, if she had enough time to make it work.

My momma told her, "You don't know who he's been hanging out with. You don't know who he owes money to, and if they show up at your door looking for him you could get hurt, too."

And Granny, seeming bigger than her small stature— she's not much over five feet tall—stood over me and said, "You can get better, Josh. You can get all the way better and get back to playing ball."

My sense of self-worth was so small it was nearly non-existent. I didn't want to hear any encouragement, and I especially didn't want to hear anything about baseball. I was so deep into a hole of self-hatred that even a mention of my past life made my insides recoil. The thought of playing baseball was about as real as the thought of me becoming president of the United States, or pope. I listened politely to Granny, though, because I could lash out against my parents and Katie and any other authority figure, but I couldn't lash out at Granny. I had retained at least that much of my humanity.

I became Granny's cause. She lived alone and filled her days with errands and television shows and conversations with family. Now, she had more than that. She had her wayward grandson in her home, and she wasn't going to let the opportunity pass without a serious effort to make it work.

The Granny plan called for me to get back on a regular schedule. She set out the rules: I couldn't go more than twelve hours without something to eat and drink; I would not be able to sleep past ten-thirty in the morning; I would go to bed at a decent hour.

Right from the start, this became an unusual partnership. She was the last refuge, and I was the refugee. When every other door closed, hers remained open. She began filling my head with positive thoughts. She talked about our family and pointed out the photos of me in my Hamilton Machine baseball uniform, curly blond hair everywhere. She talked about getting healthy, and yes, she continued to talk about baseball.

She didn't lecture me, and that's a big reason why I was there. She didn't scream at me for the decisions I had made that put me in this position. I felt comfortable and safe for the first time in a long time. I felt like I could start being myself again.

And after three days of eating and resting under Granny's roof, in the early evening of October 3, I went out and bought more crack. The addiction proved more powerful than the shame or the regret or the unconditional love of my grandma. I scrounged up some money, drove out to the trailer, and bought as much as I could.

Perhaps as a sign of my shame, or a weird pull of responsibility, I had no interest in hanging out and using at the trailer. I stopped and got a rosebud and a box of Chore Boy and drove back to Granny's house. I retreated to the back bedroom, which is separated from my grandma's bedroom by the TV room. I closed the door and, under my grandmother's roof, proceeded to get high. The rush of adrenaline filled every pore, and I was captive once again.

Within minutes of lighting up, I heard Granny outside the door.

"Josh, I smell something funny. What are you doing in there?"

Panic. It was a warm night, and my one-track mind had failed to notice the air conditioner was running. My single-minded obsession had also kept me from realizing I needed to open the bedroom window and blow the smoke through the screen.

"Nothing, Granny," I said in a tone that couldn't have been very convincing.

"Well, I smell something."

I hid the stuff and opened the door. There, about three feet from me, was Granny, standing in a blue haze of crack smoke. My heart sank. The acrid smoke blew through the vents and circulated throughout the house. Granny was watching television as the smoke started drifting under the bedroom door.

She knew. Of course she knew. But she didn't say anything more. She just looked at me with a forlorn look of hurt and disappointment—it was a look I had seen on so many faces for so many years—and went back to her television.

I felt terrible, but what did I do? I closed the door, opened the window, and took another hit.

■ ■ ■

It's difficult to explain the feeling of addiction. I can't adequately express how the desire for the next fix swarms over you and sweeps away any other desire or thought. Sitting in the den with my grandma, watching television while she encouraged me to get my life together and build my body back up to strength, I knew I had to get clean. I knew I *needed* to get clean. This knowledge was the easy part. When I thought about acting on it, though, I felt trapped and hopeless.

On October 5, I repeated the events of two days previous. I went back to the trailer, got some more crack, and returned to the back bedroom. This time I opened the window before I started and blew the smoke through the screen. I sat there by myself, the world a distant rumor, and retreated into my own altered state. I got high and stayed high, through the afternoon, into the night and straight on through morning.

Granny went about her business without bothering me. She let her rules slide. I went past twelve hours without food, past sixteen, past twenty. I was holed up for hours, doing nothing and feeling nothing. I couldn't deal with my problems, so I shut them out. In some distant part of my brain, I thought I could make those problems go away by smoking crack out of a rosebud vase packed with Chore Boy.

When I finally emerged from the room, at some time during the morning of October 6, Granny was waiting for me in the hallway. I wanted to walk past, but she wouldn't budge. My eyes met hers. I could see the tears building in her eyes as she stood there staring at the human wreckage before her. This time, though, there was something different. Along with the sadness in her eyes there was something else: anger, bordering on rage. She was determined to make this work, and I had crossed her. I had betrayed her loyalty. Worst of all, I was making everybody's prediction come true. I was proving that I couldn't be trusted, and proving that opening her door had been a mistake.

"I can't take this anymore, Josh," she said. "I can't sit here and watch you kill yourself, and I can't sit here and watch you hurt all the people who love you. We're all dying inside because of what you're doing to yourself."

Her voice was firm but not loud. She stood, almost coiled, the words measured and direct. I was defenseless, speechless. She had always been the safety net, the one person who wouldn't judge or preach. Now I could see the stark reality before me: I was in danger of losing her. Without her, I had nothing. Without this partnership, I was on the street, living for the next hit. Through the lingering haze in my brain, I could feel the buzz of shame coursing through my veins. I looked at the floor, hoping to disappear.

"You are such a good boy," she said. "There is so much good you could do with your life, and instead you're wasting it. I will not let it happen under my roof. If you're going to continue to do this, I'm kicking you out. It's your choice."

My eyes met hers. She gave me one last look with that mixture of sorrow and anger before walking away. I didn't make any promises or apologies. I didn't say anything at all, but I walked back to the room and thought about what my life had become. Who was I? I had a beautiful two-month-old daughter and a wife who had stayed with me beyond the point of reason, and I essentially gave them up to chase a high. I thought about baseball, about how good I was and how much I enjoyed the game and how much talent I had wasted.

And then I thought about my daddy, who once told me, "You know the biggest sin of this whole deal? It's you depriving the people of watching you play ball."

I had been given so much, and yet I found my life reduced to this—a series of cheap highs and a borrowed room in my grandmother's house.

This wasn't life. This wasn't living. I had lost the joy that came with being an honest man. I had lost the peace that came with having no secrets and nothing to hide. I missed the joy that came with hitting a ball and running hard, or tracking down a liner in the gap, or throwing a laser beam from center field to the plate only to see the runner from third think better of it and scurry back to the base like a mouse returning to its hole.

I missed life.

This wasn't the first time I had come to these realizations, but it was the first time some basic truths hit home. It was the first time I understood—or chose to understand—how directly and personally I was hurting the people I loved, and who loved me. For whatever reason, my grandma's words, along with the hurt in her voice and the sorrow in her eyes, were embedded in my mind as I sat in that room.

And in that room I made a decision. I made the decision to surrender. My problems were too big for me, and I concluded I could no longer kid myself into believing I could solve them by myself. I could no longer fool myself into believing I'd get around to straightening up after just one more high. I could no longer fight alone.

In the past, my response to helplessness would have been to use. Using was the all-purpose reaction, good for any occasion, suitable for any emotion. Sad? Use. Happy? Use. Angry? Use. Afraid? Use.

The problems changed, but the response never did.

This time, I began to pray. I dropped my 180-pound body to its knees and asked for help. Tears filled my eyes as I pleaded for mercy. I knew God wasn't going to come down and smooth out the world for me, but I knew I needed Him if I was to have any chance of getting through this.

I had tried the get-me-out-of-this-foxhole prayers too many times, and I knew they weren't what God wanted to hear. He didn't want that kind of relationship. This time, I wasn't trying to make a deal with God. I was admitting my weakness and telling Him I was ready to live for Him and what is right. I wanted Him to do with me what He would, whether that meant recovery or death. I would go wherever He led me, whether to redemption or to an early grave. Either one would provide relief from this lingering hell. I was at His mercy.

And as I sat there on that bed, feeling my granny's pain—no, my whole family's pain—through the walls of her house, I realized this wasn't the reason I was put on this earth. After so many years of bringing joy to people through my abilities on the baseball field, after so many years of being someone who could bring a smile to the face of a young kid at a ballpark or a young man with Down syndrome, I was now just a conveyor of pain and disappointment.

When my daddy said my biggest sin was depriving people of my ability, he was telling me that my talent wasn't strictly *my* talent. It belonged, by extension, to all the people who made a special trip to a ballpark in Florida or West Virginia or New York to watch some kid from North Carolina hit or field or throw.

There was a Bible in the room, and I picked it up and absent mindedly started thumbing through the pages. I read a few verses and moved on. I didn't know what I was looking for, or, really, that I was looking for anything at all, but I ran across a verse—James 4:7—that caught my attention.

> *Humble yourself before God. Resist the devil and he will flee from you.*

I read that over and over, committing it to memory. I vowed to change, to make every move from here on a positive one. I battled vicious physical cravings—the devil coming at me hard—and as soon as I felt one coming on I would repeat the verse.

With God and Granny by my side, I white-knuckled my way through the first week. The cravings were impossible to ignore. My hands got clammy and cold, and then my palms would start sweating. *Humble yourself before God*...Smells got to me. I would pass a burger place while driving with the window down and it would remind me of the smell of crack. *Humble yourself before God*...Everything became a reminder, whether it was a smell or a sight or something that took place entirely in my head. *Humble yourself before God*...A restaurant reminded me of drinking, or scoring drugs from someone on the staff.

I started coughing up black stuff, tar-black crack soot, out of my lungs. I would cough and cough, then spit out chunks of black sputum that must have been caked to my lungs. It was like I'd worked in a coal mine all my life.

I spoke to the devil. He came at me with cravings, tempting me to yield to his evil power. I convinced myself the cravings were nothing more than thoughts—thoughts created by the devil—and out loud I told him, "These are just thoughts. I am not going to act on them." The physical act of voicing their existence and then dismissing them emboldened me. I spoke to the devil. It gave me a measure of control.

Through it all, Granny stood beside me. She was my confidante, pushing positive thoughts on me the way Murd pushed crack. She cooked me good ol' country dishes—steak and mashed potatoes with gravy, pork chops and biscuits with squash. She cooked me breakfast every morning. Most mornings, the first thing that hit me after Granny woke me up was the smell of bacon making its way into the back room.

"How you feeling today, Josh?" she asked most mornings.

"Not too bad, Granny," I'd answer.

"You ready for your bacon and eggs?"

I'd been sober for less than a week when I had my first bad dream. When I was using, I never dreamed. If I slept, it was the deep, dreamless sleep of a stalled brain. It was the sleep of the dead.

This dream caused me to wake in a panic, covered

in sweat. It was 3:00 A.M., and it took me a few seconds to take inventory of my situation. I had slept in so many places and awakened in so many different stages of disorientation that I needed to run down a checklist.

In my grandma's house. *Check.* Safe. *Check.* Sober. *Check.*

Grandma's house is rural, not quite country, but the nights carry the kind of dead silence that fills a room. I was suddenly aware of the silence, and the vivid scenes from my dream were a physical presence.

In the dream, I was fighting the devil. He wasn't the classic red, horned beast, though. He was a man, a large unsmiling man who was terrifying in his intensity. It was the same vision I had seen in the clouds above the stadium in West Virginia six years before. In the dream I was holding a stick, or maybe a baseball bat, and I kept hitting him and he kept getting back up. I would swing my hardest and knock down the devil, but over and over he got back up. My best shot couldn't wipe him out.

Eventually, I became exhausted. My swings got slower and less powerful, and just as it appeared the devil would overpower my wrung-out body, I woke up.

The dream hung with me. I couldn't dismiss the vision of the devil as a gross distortion of an ordinary man. I tried to get back to sleep, to ignore the dream lingering in my head and the silence bearing down on me from all four walls. I had never felt more alone.

I had been alone for so long. All the time I was using, I was alone with the fears and the sadness and the emotions I worked so hard to kill with the drugs. But now I was truly alone, fighting the urge to use but afraid of what reality might bring. I had no idea how hard this might get, and no idea what might come next.

I got up and sat on the edge of the bed. *Humble yourself before God.* I looked around the room and tried to calm myself. It was no use. The loneliness scared me. I got up and opened the door and walked out of the bedroom and through my grandma's television room.

I stood at the closed door of Granny's bedroom. I was a twenty-four-year-old man, a former professional athlete, the number-one pick, the $4 million man.

I knocked gently, opened the door, and walked in.

"Slide over, Granny," I said. "I'm scared."

■ ■ ■

My weight rose from 180 to 205 within weeks. My ribs were filling in. My shoulders and legs were gaining strength, even though I wasn't doing anything but eating and avoiding drugs. The black soot in my lungs turned gray, then disappeared altogether. The dream stayed away.

I brought a scale into the bedroom and weighed myself every morning. Granny kept waking me up to get food into me. I had been sober only a short time, but this time felt different. When I surrendered to God, He took care of the rest. I had a peacefulness inside me, a calm that I hadn't felt since I started using. I took a quick inventory every morning. Sober? Yes. Safe? Yes. That was all I needed. From there I set out to make that day as positive as I could. There were so many mornings I woke up disoriented, not even knowing where I was. I can't begin to explain the simple pleasure that came with going to bed at a decent hour and waking up at a decent hour knowing I hadn't hurt myself or anybody else the night before.

Word spread to the family first, then beyond. *Granny*

*says Josh hasn't used for two weeks now. I saw Josh the other day
and he looks pretty good. I saw Granny at the store and she says
she can't buy enough food to feed that boy.*

I couldn't do this on my own. I prayed that Jesus would
lead me to the right path, and I believed in the power of
being positive. Granny told me every day how good I
looked, and as the scale inched up I even started to believe
her. It seemed the only two people who believed I could
be salvaged were in this house.

I had been sober about three weeks when Granny
looked at me shoveling food into my mouth and said,
"You know what, Josh?"

"What, Granny?"

"You're doing this, Josh. You're really doing it."

Between forkfuls, I said, "No, you're wrong, Granny.
We're doing it."

She got up from her chair and turned to the sink, pretending to be interested in the dishes.

"It's all you, Josh," she said quietly, wiping away a tear.

■ ■ ■

About this time, Granny started talking about baseball as
if it were a foregone conclusion. She'd just mention it in
passing, something like, "When you get back to playing
ball..." Or sometimes she'd say, "You can still play ball,
Josh. You're a young man, and once this is all behind you,
you'll get back to it."

I listened, but I didn't really believe. I desperately wanted
to play again, and I desperately missed it, but I felt so defeated
that I couldn't bear any more disappointment. I remembered my daddy telling me how I deprived everybody of

seeing my talent, and I remembered Katie telling me how God spoke to her and said I'd be back playing baseball for a cause bigger than the game.

But it didn't compute. Not yet, anyway. I was off the hamster wheel, and for now that was enough. I was still figuring out how to get better, and it was a monumental task. I was doing this for me, not for baseball, and I needed to keep it that way. It was overwhelming to think about dealing with my addiction while getting ready to play baseball again. That felt like scaling Everest and seeing Kilimanjaro sitting on top of it.

Who would take a chance on me? How would I be received if someone did? As soon as those questions popped into my head, I had to get them out. Too much, too soon.

It was easier to just give up on baseball, or at least put it aside. Priorities—life first, baseball second.

Then one day Granny was doing the dishes and I was sitting at the table eating—it seemed like I was always eating. "Granny," I said. "I don't think I'm ever going to play baseball again."

FOURTEEN

GRANNY KNEW. As soon as I told her I didn't see myself playing baseball again, she turned back to her dishes and smiled to herself. Why was she smiling? I wasn't telling her something she wanted to hear, and yet she responded as if I had relayed good news. What was she thinking behind that smile?

Along with being headstrong, Granny is observant, and she smiled because it was the first time I brought up baseball on my own. "This meant you were *thinking* about ball," she told me later. "And that's when I knew you'd get back to *playing* ball." She'd been waiting for that moment.

When it came to baseball, she was persistent. She worked me, filling me with positive thoughts, but she never pushed me so far that I'd push back. Every once in a while she'd tell me again that it wasn't too late, and as the clean days rolled from one into the next she picked up the pace, sometimes finishing sentences about the future with "...but that'll be when you're playing ball again." She was subtle, and she was smart.

I know she missed watching me play, and being around her day and night like this made me realize how much hurt I'd caused and how much promise I'd wasted.

And the truth was, I thought about baseball all the time, even if I didn't talk about it. Since the suspensions started, the game had become something of a millstone around my neck. It was always around when someone wanted to remind me of who I'd once been. From the moment I surrendered and asked God for guidance, I began seeing myself in the clearest possible terms: I was a guy with a serious problem, who needed to solve that problem to save his life, not his baseball career.

I needed to get clean for me, not for baseball. I needed to trust God and see my way out of addiction, not tease myself into believing baseball would ever be an option again.

Think about it: I'd made a solid effort to destroy my body for nearly four years straight, and I had no idea what kind of damage I'd done. The only running I'd done was out of desperation. I hadn't picked up a ball in months. I hadn't swung at anything but a windshield in just as long. Since I found crack, my body had deteriorated to the point of being unrecognizable.

I didn't know if my eyes still worked or if my legs still worked or if I could even swing a bat. Honestly, I was afraid to find out. I was coughing crack soot out of my lungs and fighting off persistent cravings that had my palms sweating like they'd sprung a leak. I was supposed to think about running around the bases and tracking down a bullet hit to the alley in right-center?

To come back to be a good husband, father, and man of God, I needed to be clean and I needed to be responsible. I had shown signs of being able to regain that part of myself. But baseball was an entirely different animal. To come back and play baseball I would need to do more than be able to build up my weight and stay civil to the people around me and give all the glory to God. Playing baseball meant building my body back to the point where I could be a professional athlete, and that was just too much to think about at this stage of the game.

I was a crack addict, in the early, early stages of recovery. That's all I was, and all I could pretend to be. Reality first. In this condition, baseball had to remain a rumor. Professional baseball? Way past the horizon. And major-league baseball? That exceeded the limits of imagination.

But good things were happening. Small, good things. By the end of October, my coughing slowed and the black stuff disappeared. The dark rings under my eyes were less noticeable. My face started filling out, and I no longer looked like a skeleton wrapped in skin. The dead look in my blue eyes was replaced by something resembling the person I used to be.

I was broken, but I was healing. Piece by piece, I was healing.

Every morning Granny would tell me how well I was doing, and how good I looked. I had surrendered to God, but I never asked for Him to heal me. But there was no denying something was happening inside me, both physically and spiritually. My faith in Jesus grew, and my faith in myself grew along with it.

October became November, and every day got easier. I could feel the pounds and the strength gradually return to my body. I was eating grits and grilled cheese sandwiches and pizza. I was drinking sweet tea the way I'd always liked it—a little tea with my sugar, thank you—and enjoying the freedom that came with staring down my demons by taking a deep breath and saying a prayer till the craving went away.

Piece by piece.

And it wasn't just physical. Granny decided to trust me with her credit card, a move that would have led her directly to financial ruin a mere six weeks before. Since I showed up at her door, though, I had earned back bits of her trust. Six weeks previously, I was a guy whose wife was moving and hiding money like someone running a three-card monte game on a Manhattan street corner. Now I was being trusted with a credit card. It was intended only for me to buy pizza over the phone, but still.

Piece by piece.

There were days I would eat three meals and then mix in a pizza late in the evening. I would order it to be delivered, and I always left the receipt on the kitchen table so Granny could see what I'd bought with her money. She didn't require a receipt, but it made me feel good to be someone who could be trusted again, and to prove I could be responsible in return.

Piece by piece.

I started walking around a little bit, just across the property and over to the cemetery and around to the old places I'd traveled to a million times as a kid. It felt good to breathe deeply without coughing, and for the first time in several years I felt the beginning of the crisp fall air and believed it was the start of something good.

I enjoyed the solitude. It gave me time to think about priorities and to organize my thoughts. I started to miss Katie and Julia and wonder about my baby girl, Sierra. Mostly, the solitude gave me the chance to slow down and let my body and mind catch up after the years of aimless running.

Piece by piece.

I caught myself laughing and smiling spontaneously. I could react to things around me without suspicion or paranoia. I stopped thinking everybody was out to get me and started to see people for what they were. Ever since I had seen the look of hurt in Granny's eyes, I told God I didn't want to cause any more pain. I had caused enough, and I was ready to move forward.

To do that, I couldn't allow myself to be consumed by guilt. I took responsibility for what I'd done, but it wasn't healthy to live in guilt and regret. I wouldn't blame anyone but me, but I would no longer beat myself up over what I'd done and who I'd hurt.

Piece by piece.

Christmas neared. I went out and bought small gifts for Katie, Julia, and Sierra. I called Katie and asked her if she and the girls would be willing to meet with me so I could give them their gifts. She wasn't ready to have me visit the house, so we agreed to meet in the parking lot of a Food Barn, where I held Sierra and hugged Katie and wished them merry Christmas and drove away with tears running down my cheeks.

Piece by piece.

One day I put on some workout clothes and walked down to the shop my grandfather had built between my childhood home and Granny's house. I unlocked the door and flipped on the light and stood looking at the Bowflex machine I had brought here from the Garner house about a year earlier.

I swiped the dust off the bench and sat down. I did a few sets, got my heart rate climbing (in a natural way, a welcome change), and sat there smiling to myself. My stamina was about what I'd expected, but my strength was not too bad.

My goal was to be positive. I had been positive with my mind, so it seemed natural to take the next step and be positive with my body. It felt good to strain my muscles for the first time in a long, long time, and it felt good to expand my lungs and breathe hard at the end of a set.

The next day my chest and arms were sore. Soreness never felt so good.

Piece by piece.

This was another step, another small but positive step. I was taking them regularly now, one at a time. I didn't know where they would lead, but I felt pulled in a positive direction with the same force that had led me astray. This time, however, there was an importance difference.

I was sure there was a different director in charge.

■ ■ ■

While I was at my grandmother's house, putting the pieces together, Katie was having an ordeal of her own. She was trying to come to terms with her anger. I don't think either of us had it easy.

The ripples of my addiction spread in concentric circles, and Katie was in the first circle. She got the tallest waves and the most severe swells.

The emotions ran through her. She went from angry to sad to disgusted to bitter to vengeful to resigned and then back to angry again. She would sit home, wondering where I was, trying to convince herself she didn't care. Then she would realize she did care, she cared deeply, and her frustration at not knowing whether she would ever see me alive would start the cycle all over again.

It wasn't healthy. My troubles were consuming her, taking over her life. She needed direction. She needed someone to tell her to leave me or embrace me or forget about me. She called our pastor, Jimmy Carroll, and his wife.

"Jimmy and Beverly, I need to talk to you." Her voice quivered on the phone. "I won't lie to you, I'm mad. I'm angry. Josh should be reprimanded for what he's done. He can't treat people this way and expect to get away with it."

They invited her over to their house. When she got there, they ushered her to the living room. They listened to her vent about my failings and her feelings. She told them I was making progress, but how could she trust me to stay clean? How could she allow herself to be drawn back in, knowing disappointment was a distinct possibility?

Finally, Katie said, "I need to know what God wants me to do."

Jimmy folded his hands in front of him and said, "I can tell you're angry, and you might not like what I'm about to say."

Katie just looked at him, wanting to know what she should do. More than anything, I think, she wanted to know if there was anything she *could* do.

Jimmy said, "You know what God wants you to do, don't you?"

"No, that's why I'm here."

"Katie, God wants you to forgive Josh."

Katie had all this anger, all this frustration, all this resentment. All those worried phone calls that went straight to voicemail. All those nights spent sitting up waiting for me, knowing I wasn't planning on coming home. All that time sitting around wondering whether to give up on me or give me one more last chance.

The bitterness needed to go somewhere, didn't it? It needed an outlet. It needed to get out and breathe, and now she was told to swallow it? To let it go? To forgive?

To her, forgiveness sounded like a cop-out. It sounded like letting me off the hook.

And yet, deep inside, she knew Jimmy was right.

He was looking at her, for who knows how long, waiting for a response.

"Forgive?" Katie asked.

"Not just forgive," Jimmy said. "Forgive completely."

It took some time for Katie to digest this advice. I was someone who had turned her life upside-down time and again, to the point where she needed to get a restraining order against me just to make sure I didn't come around when she was trying to sell our house. And the advice she got from her spiritual leaders was not only forgive, but forgive completely? She'd waited a long time to give me what I had coming to me—I'm sure it had been planned and replanned in her head a million times—and now she was told that Jesus would forgive and forget. Forgive and forget and not mention it ever again. She shook her head but accepted it. How hard was that?

They sat and prayed about it. Jimmy and Beverly knew it wouldn't be easy, but they knew it wouldn't work any other way. I hadn't responded to any of the thousands of attempts to scare or berate me into getting clean, so chances were that confronting me would be a waste of time, anyway. And even if it made Katie feel better to get it off her chest and let me know how many different ways I had failed her, the effort might backfire.

Over the course of her visit, Katie traveled the distance from bitterness to understanding. She thanked them for their time and left. On the drive home, she told God she would forgive me completely, but she hoped for something in return. She wanted to be free of all the feelings of resentment. Forgiving was the right thing to do, but she couldn't forgive and still harbor the resentment that she felt. That would kill her, and kill any chance of repairing our relationship.

She had lost her husband. She had come home from the hospital with our new baby—an event that is supposed to be one of the happiest of a person's life—and found only worry and fear. She found an unthinkable environment where she could send her husband out for a bottle of medicine and not see or hear from him for three or four days. She was raising Julia and Sierra by herself, and her inability to understand why I insisted on self-destructing rather than being with people who loved and cared for me was more than she could bear.

And now all she wanted was freedom from those feelings, in the same way I wanted freedom from the shackles of my drug use.

When Katie got home from the pastor's house, she picked up the phone and called my grandma's house. She asked to speak to me, not knowing whether I was going to pick up the phone.

When I answered, she got right to the point. "Josh, I just want you to know that I forgive you. And I also want you to know that I won't hold anything you've done against you from now on. If you can keep getting better and we can work to reconcile our relationship, I promise not to bring any of this stuff up again."

My body was adjusting to the shock of getting off drugs. I was filling my days with positive thoughts to offset the cravings that rocked me and made my palms sweat in an air-conditioned room. I was making progress. I spent my days praying for the strength to string together one more good day, just one more good day. And those days were building.

My surrender to God's will, and my plea for His help, led me to an understanding of the nature of this fight. As Katie's father once told me, I would reach a point where it was do or die. I would either get better, or die. When I walked up the path to my grandma's front door, I had reached that fork in the road.

When Katie finished, I offered only a quiet "Thank you" before hanging up, but her call came at a crucial time. Granny filled my head with positive thoughts throughout the day, and now Katie was offering her unconditional forgiveness. I had become accustomed to the opposite approach, to people reminding me constantly what a disappointment I was to them.

These new attitudes—mine, theirs—gave me not just faint flickers of hope, but rays of hope. I didn't want to jinx it, but I closed my eyes that night and repeated the verse that had become my new mantra:

Humble yourself before God. Resist the devil and he will flee from you.

And once again, I let the thought creep into my head: *I think I can do this.*

FIFTEEN

GRADUALLY, I MADE my way back into the world. Big Daddy, my father-in-law, put me in touch with a psychiatrist at Duke University named Dr. Keith Brodie. Dr. Brodie was the former head of the school's psychiatry department as well as the former president and chancellor of the school. Big Daddy knew him, and he believed I could be helped by sitting down and talking to him.

From the moment Dr. Brodie and I had our first conversation, I felt a connection with him that I hadn't felt with any other doctor. He knew the mind of an addict, and he knew the mind of an athlete, and our sessions were immensely productive.

Dr. Brodie understood one undeniable fact about my life to this point: I got into trouble when I didn't have baseball. It was the catch-22 of my problem: Without baseball, I had little reason to stop using; while I was using, I would never be allowed to return to baseball.

So, with repeated suspensions lining up around me like prison walls, I had trouble seeing a way out. Whenever I got clean before, for stretches up to four or maybe five months, I would end up looking down the road and seeing another six months before I could even apply for reinstatement to play again. The road was long, and my patience was short.

But now, with my sobriety unconnected to baseball, I felt how quickly my body seemed to be bouncing back. I was encouraged, and a little bit amazed, every time I started to do something physical. I knew there would be physical repercussions from the years of drug abuse, things like a compromised immune system that led to suscepti-bility to any kind of infection, but for now, this soon after quitting, I felt better than I had a right to feel.

With Dr. Brodie's urging, I started to think the unthinkable.

Could I really get back in the game?

I received a call from Marc Topkin of the *St. Petersburg Times*. He covered the Devil Rays, and he heard through team channels that I was doing better and getting clean. And by the way, what about baseball?

I'd been through this so many times I didn't want to get anybody's hopes too high. Not my family's, not the Devil Rays', and certainly not mine. I wanted to make the point that I was feeling better. This time felt different. This time felt real.

That seemed like enough.

But inside me, thoughts of baseball accelerated. It was my job, the only thing I'd really done for any length of time. I thought back to my daddy's words—"Your big-gest sin is depriving people of watching you play"—and wondered what I'd be like now. Could I still be, in Dad-dy's words, "the best the game's ever seen"?

And how would I ever know if I didn't give it a shot?

■ ■ ■

The story appeared in the *St. Petersburg Times,* informing the baseball world I had once again begun thinking about resuscitating my baseball career. That afternoon, the phone rang and Granny handed it to me, shrugging her shoulders to tell me she had no idea who it was.

"Josh, this is Roy Silver. My partner Randy Holland and I run a baseball facility in Clearwater called the Winning Inning. We saw the story in the paper this morning and we'd like to offer you a place to stay and a place to work out."

I listened to Roy explain his philosophy. The Winning Inning was a Christ-centered baseball facility that ran programs for ballplayers from little kids to major-leaguers. The motto was "Developing Players from the Inside Out," which seemed about right for me. It was located in Clearwater at the old Phillies' spring training site, Jack Russell Stadium.

He was offering me one of the old Phillies' minorleague offices to sleep in, and his facility to work out in, but it wasn't a handout. I would be required to work around the facility—doing jobs that ranged from raking the field to cleaning toilets—to earn time in the batting cage or on the field.

Roy tracked me down at Granny's house because he had seen the story in the paper and he knew of me from his days as a Devil Rays' minor-league coach. He was offering me what amounted to a stay at a ballplayer's halfway house, and right away it sounded like the perfect opportunity for me.

This was another example of God providing for me. When events line up the way they did, logic doesn't explain them. And if not logic, then what?

When I got off the phone with Roy Silver, I really

started thinking about the course of events for the past couple of months. From the moment I had wobbled to Granny's screen door to being offered a place to get back in baseball shape under the eyes of two Christian men with my best interests at heart, I could only say the logic of it all continued to escape me.

I came to the only "logical" conclusion.

It was a God thing.

In a way, I didn't think I could turn down the opportunity. When I surrendered, my exact words were, "Do with me what you want." This seemed like another God-sent message that I needed to accept in order to fulfill my mission.

Katie and I discussed the opportunity, and we agreed it would be a perfect next step in my progress. After further discussions, I became more comfortable with Roy and Randy, and the idea of starting over in a quiet, low-key atmosphere without any crazy expectations appealed to me.

About this time, Katie came down with a horrible case of the flu. She called me and I went over to the house and took her to the hospital. I took care of Sierra and Julia while Katie was laid up, and holding Sierra in my arms with the knowledge that I'd been given a second chance to be a good father made me resolve to make that work, too.

A couple of days later, I came down with the flu just as Katie was starting to feel better, so the roles were reversed and she took care of me. The few days we spent taking care of each other convinced us our relationship was worth fighting for, and we agreed on a course of action. I would go to the Winning Inning, work on baseball and recovery, and then we would work on repairing our relationship.

We made a commitment to each other. It was a commitment I wouldn't have been able to make without first making the commitment to myself.

My life was coming together.

On January 17, 2006, three and a half months after I showed up at Granny's doorstep, I left Raleigh and headed for Tampa, to take a shot at resuming my baseball career.

Piece by piece.

Before I left, I wrote a letter to Granny, sealed it in an envelope, and left it on the kitchen table. I hugged her and thanked her, and I told her I would never forget what she did for me.

In the letter, I wrote:

People talk about tough love, but you showed me true love.

■ ■ ■

Nobody could say I was spoiled. At the Winning Inning, I slept on an air mattress in an old upstairs office formerly used by some long-gone Phillies manager. I showered in an old clubhouse and hung my clothes in an open locker. I did not feel like a pampered athlete.

Every day I cleaned toilets and mopped floors and raked the fields. Roy and Randy kept an eye on me, but they gave me my space. I did my work throughout the day to earn time in the batting cage in the evening. I worked out and ran and tested my body for the first time since I got clean.

There were worries about how I would handle my freedom—or, more like semifreedom—this time around. My parents were worried, Katie was worried. Their worries were understandable, but I left with a newfound confidence and calm. I wasn't venturing back into the world alone this time; I had God on my side, guiding me to make the right decisions. I began every day with a prayer asking for the strength to make that day positive, to end the day as a better man, husband, and father than I was when I woke up.

Roy and Randy ran after-school camps and other group activities for kids in the area. It was part of their mission, using baseball as their ministry. This became one of my favorite things about the place. Being around the little kids reignited my love for baseball and made me realize why I had to give myself another chance to get back into the game. I saw them and I saw myself, a kid who lived for the game and had no worries. I saw myself at a time when I didn't have bad thoughts, when my life was simpler and baseball was fun and easy and worry-free.

There was one boy in particular, a twelve-year-old named Julius, who lived across the street in a tough neighborhood with his great-grandmother. We had very little in common—Julius was a street-smart black kid who had seen more than his share of hardship—but we bonded over baseball.

Julius had only been playing baseball for a year or two at this point, and he came to the Winning Inning almost every day after school to hit and work out. He played on one of the teams sponsored by the facility, and he could really play.

Baseball just happened to be the opportunity presented to Julius. Roy and Randy made it available to him, and it was a safe place for him to spend the afternoon. They made sure he brought his schoolwork, and they gave him chores to teach him responsibility.

Julius showed his gratitude on the field. He played with abandon, loving every minute of it. I would watch him and just smile, seeing the game for the first time again as I watched him run around like I used to, treating the diamond as his own playground.

My life probably looked pretty good to him. I was living in a clubhouse, working for the right to play. Most twelve-year-olds who live in an environment where people are selling drugs off their apartment stoop would think this was the life.

Julius started coming to our Tuesday night Bible study, and that's where he learned a little bit of my story. He started looking up to me, and there were many times when I was hitting in the cage, thinking I was all alone, only to turn around and see Julius's wide smile and adoring eyes staring at me. Usually he was shaking his head, amazed at the speed and sound of the ball coming off my bat.

He didn't judge me or question me. I told him I had made mistakes, and I told him he didn't have to give in to the same temptations that got me. His life was hard, and there were obstacles that I didn't face, but I tried to tell him that God and baseball were two pretty good ways to keep himself out of trouble.

He listened to what I had to say, and he watched everything I did. I can't explain how much this meant to me at this stage of my recovery. After so many years of disappointing people, of trying and failing, seeing someone respond to my ability like this was yet another sign that I was back on track. I've always fed off the response I've gotten from the way I swing the bat, but his smile and look of wonderment was something I felt in my soul. When I saw Julius, I saw Jesus working through him.

More than just about anything, this strengthened my resolve to get back into the game. It reinforced the idea that I was doing the right thing, in the right place. I remembered Katie's words, way back when hope was hard to find. *You're going to be back playing baseball. Josh, there's a bigger plan for you. When you come back, it's going to be about more than baseball.* If I had any doubts, this erased them. I was sent here to use baseball as a platform for something bigger. This was my calling.

One night at the Winning Inning I had a dream that I was competing in the Home Run Derby at the All-Star Game. At this stage of my recovery, this was a pretty far-out dream. I was hitting well and everybody was cheering, but I wasn't keeping count of how many I hit. I couldn't place the stadium or the pitcher, but when it was over someone called me over toward the dugout, where I stood to be interviewed by a female television reporter. I woke up on my air mattress in the old manager's office feeling happy and wondering, How many home runs did I hit? Did I win? I didn't know how many, and I didn't know whether I won or lost. And I realized there was a reason: God doesn't care about winning or losing. It's not important; what's important is to be there, and to use your gifts to the fullest potential.

■　■　■

Every year there's a college baseball spring tournament at the Jack Russell complex. Teams from the cold-weather states come down to Florida to play some early season games and enjoy some decent weather. To me, this meant I had to get to work. I needed to help prepare the fields and the facility to host the tournament. Bullpen mounds, bathrooms, bleachers—everything had to be cleaned up and spruced up.

On the first day of the tournament, Penn State and Ohio State were on the field getting ready to play each other. I was walking around in my Timberland boots and cargo shorts, carrying a rake to get the bullpens in shape.

I was in the Penn State bullpen, watching their pitchers scuffle and goof around and generally waste time in the traditional way baseball players have been doing for more than a hundred years. They weren't doing much; I think it was five or six hours before the game. We were talking back and forth, about not much of anything, when I noticed one of their catchers was standing there, in full gear.

I nodded toward him.

"Hey, can I throw a couple?"

They had no idea who I was. I was just a guy working on a field. They might have thought I'd be good for a laugh, so one of them said, "Why not?"

I had been throwing for a couple of weeks by this point, so I wasn't in midseason form by any means. My arm, though, had been feeling pretty good.

I borrowed a glove and tossed a few to get loose. Then I backed up to the mound and told the catcher to get into his squat.

After two pitches, their eyes were wide and they were looking at me like I was something they'd never seen before. A few of them were sitting on the bench to the side of the mound, where the ball whizzed by them. "I can hear that thing," one of them said.

Timberland boots, cargo shorts—to them, I was like the guy from *The Rookie* or something.

When I was finished, I tossed the ball to one of the guys and went back to my rake.

"Hey, can you come in and close for us today?" one of the guys asked.

"I wish I could," I said. "You have no idea how much I wish I could."

■ ■ ■

Katie and I were in constant contact while I was in Clear-water, and she decided to leave the girls with her parents and make a trip down to see me. Circumstances had kept us apart physically, but I felt we were growing closer together from a distance. Now it was time for us to give our reconciliation a chance to work in person.

The first day she arrived was the day she watched me take batting practice for the first time. She had never seen me compete, ever, and her reaction—"If I had known you were throwing away *that* kind of talent, I would have been so much angrier with you"—is something we still laugh about.

The time we spent away gave us each time to reflect and take stock of our relationship. We were committed to making it work, and from the moment we were together in Clear-water it felt as if none of those bad times ever happened.

Katie made a promise not to throw my past back at me, and she kept it.

I made a promise to be positive every day, to wake up every morning intent on making myself a better husband, father, and man of faith. I don't know whether I succeeded every day, but I certainly tried.

I was back to 235 pounds, which meant I had regained fifty pounds in less than three months. The ball was jumping off my bat, just like the old days, and I had a new-found appreciation for the game that I had given up hope of recapturing.

I was at peace. So much forgiveness had come my way, and so much mercy. I felt free to pursue my dreams once again, this time under vastly different circumstances. The expectations of being the next big thing had gone away. I had receded from the public consciousness, and any success from this point forward would be a surprise to everybody but me.

This was beginning to feel like a miracle. The cravings still hit me occasionally, but I adopted an eight-second rule when it came to bad thoughts. In recovery, I had been taught that any thought that stays in your mind for more than eight seconds can result in action. So whenever those thoughts crept into my mind, I started counting and erased the thought before I reached eight.

The more I played, the more confident I got. I was continually amazed by my body's ability to bounce back, and I stopped trying to come up with explanations. Logic played no part in any of this, and I started to shrug and say, "It's a God thing," whenever someone asked. It was the only answer I knew.

I started to believe I could do this. The game was back inside me, and I needed to make a statement to Major League Baseball that I was serious about my commitment to the game. I needed them to take notice of me and understand I was more than a name on the suspended list.

But if I couldn't play in the minor leagues, what were my options? There was really only one—independent-league baseball. These are teams unaffiliated with big-league organizations, and they are traditionally last-chance outposts for players trying to hang on to their dreams.

Richard Davis, my friend from my days in Charleston in 2000, had become a part owner of an independent team called the Brockton Rox, near Boston. He was a successful real-estate man who cohosted the A&E television show *Flip This House*. Richard suggested I try to get the Devil Rays and Major League Baseball to sign off on my playing for his team, since we figured the suspension applied only to teams officially under the MLB umbrella.

Richard and Steve Reed, my business manager, who was now working as my de facto agent, thought it would be worth a shot to go up there and play. At the very least, it would show the people in the commissioner's office that I was serious about resuming my career and staying clean.

This was May 2006, and I had been clean for seven months, the longest stretch of sobriety I had achieved since I started using back in early 2002. I had owned up to my mistakes and taken positive steps to become a man of faith and honor.

The only thing missing, it seemed to me, was the ability to go back out on the field and earn a living at the game I was born to play. As I've said a million times, baseball was really the only thing I've ever been really, really good at doing. I was ready for the game to come back into my life full-time. In fact, I needed it.

Katie and I made the decision: We would take the kids and move up there. I could work out in a batting cage in a town called Wrentham and wait for Major League Baseball to rule on my appeal. It was unclear whether my suspension applied to independent-league teams, but I wanted to go through the proper channels. The last thing I needed was to be seen as a renegade.

Knowing this was a big step, one that could create heartbreak if it didn't work out, Katie and I prayed on our decision. In the end, we felt it was a chance worth taking, and I hoped my willingness to move my family up there for a chance to play again would emphasize my dedication to the game.

The next step was to convince the decision-makers that I was a changed man. The Devil Rays wrote a letter to Commissioner Bud Selig. My father-in-law, Big Daddy, had written two letters to Selig and received polite replies each time. He wrote another letter in support of me.

Most important, Dr. Brodie wrote a letter to Selig recommending I be reinstated by MLB to pursue my career. He wrote that a return to the game could go a long way toward helping my recovery.

The final letter had to come from me. I knew everything I wanted to say, but I needed to organize my thoughts and make sure I said everything the right way. This felt like a monumental task, but it got easier when I made a decision: I would write it from the heart.

I sat down and wrote about where I'd been and where I was now, and how my life changed when I didn't have baseball. I took responsibility for my failings and asked only for a chance. I told them I truly believed everything that happened to me was part of a bigger plan, and now the plan called for me to return to the game.

I wrote that baseball was the third and final piece to my recovery, behind God and family. If I could only return to the game, if I could only get a chance to make up for the sin of denying myself and others the benefit of my talent, I could complete this circle.

We were asking MLB to bend the rules for me. By the letter of the law, I should have remained suspended and on the restricted list through the end of the 2006 season. But I felt my circumstances were extraordinary, and I was willing to play independent-league baseball for next to nothing to see if I could get back on the field.

This argument was a last-chance argument. I wanted the decision-makers to know that my sobriety was different this time around, that it was a choice made for me and my family, with God's guidance. My previous attempts at sobriety had been intended to make someone else happy, or to help my chances of getting back into baseball so I could stop being such a disappointment to everybody.

This time, I honestly thought baseball was just the final piece of the puzzle. It was a means to an end, and not the end itself.

For the first time in a long time, I felt hopeful about getting back in the game.

I knew the call would come from the Devil Rays, thumbs up or thumbs down. Now all that was left was to wait by the phone.

I told Katie the call was coming, and I told her I felt good about it. She told me not to get my hopes too high, for fear they'd be dashed and I'd be worse than when I started.

Every day we waited seemed like a week. We were taking Sierra to the pediatrician's office to get her ears checked one afternoon—June 20, 2006, to be exact—when my cell phone rang. We had just gotten out of the truck to get Sierra out of her car seat when my cell phone rang. I saw the 813 area code come up on the caller ID.

"This is it," I told Katie.

She didn't say anything, but she prayed to herself, *Please, God, let this be it.*

I took a deep breath, shot Katie a hopeful glance, and answered.

It was Andrew Friedman, the Devil Rays' general manager.

"Josh, you sitting down?"

"Is it that bad?"

"No, it's that good."

He didn't have to say anything else. I knew exactly what that meant—I was back. Not only was I back, but the commissioner's office decided if they were going to reinstate me to play independent-league baseball, they might as well allow me to return to the Devil Rays. I was being allowed to report to the Devil Rays' extended spring training in Tampa, with the idea of returning to the minor leagues at some point before the end of the season.

The biggest chill I've ever felt ran through my entire body. Katie knew immediately from the look on my face. I started crying, and I cried and laughed and tried to make sense of it all.

Katie started crying, and in the middle of a pediatrician's parking lot we stood there and made a scene — crying and laughing and hugging and bouncing around like schoolkids.

One more chance. One more last chance. God had given me new life and presented me with a miracle.

I was back in the game.

I stood there looking at my wife and baby. The tears rolled down my cheeks and lost themselves in my smile.

I was proof that hope is never lost.

■   ■   ■

A few weeks after my reinstatement, the devil reappeared in my dreams.

It was the same dream. I kept hitting the devil with a bat or a club and he kept bouncing back, rearing up at me with his hideous, cold face. He seemed unbeatable, unstoppable.

Just as I felt my strength wane and my resolve weaken — just as the devil was about to win — I felt a presence by my side. I turned and saw Jesus, fighting beside me, fighting *with* me, and suddenly I was filled with the strength of a thousand men.

We kept fighting, and finally I struck the devil and he did not reappear.

He stayed down.

We had won.

■ ■ ■

I arrived at extended spring training with the bare minimum of equipment. I had spikes and a glove, but very little else. Before the first day of workouts, my business manager, Steve Reed, called my old friend Carl Crawford of the Devil Rays and arranged to drive over to Tropicana Field to pick up a few of Carl's bats so I would have my own bats to use during batting practice.

Extended spring training is for guys recovering from injuries, or sometimes young players who need more work than they'll get on a minor-league team. I don't know where I fit in—I was, as usual, in my own category—but I was thrilled to be playing baseball for the first time in four long years.

After about a month of twice-daily workouts in Tampa, the Devil Rays assigned me to the Hudson Valley Renegades of the New York–Penn League. The team that represented my first promotion—from Rookie League in Princeton, West Virginia—was now the first stop on my new adventure.

The night I arrived in New York, I drove directly to an empty Dutchess Stadium in the town of Wappingers Falls. I looked out onto that field and remembered playing there as a kid, a lifetime ago. This time, it looked different. It looked new. Before, Hudson Valley was just a stop along the way, two words on the back of my baseball card.

This time, it stood for so much more. This time, it stood for the chance I never thought I'd get.

I walked down the right-field line and onto the field. I took off my shoes and socks and left them near the foul line. I started walking until I reached center field. I stood there in the dark, looking toward home plate, feeling the blades of grass under my feet.

■ ■ ■

The next night, my name was on the lineup card.

I put on a game uniform for the first time in longer than I could remember. I made sure everything was perfect, and I checked myself in the mirror without shame. The kids on the team looked at me with a mixture of awe and curiosity. I told them I'd played there before, what seemed like a lifetime ago.

It almost didn't matter how I did. I had proved to myself I could make it back, that I could turn one positive day into a whole stream of positive days. And all those positive days could combine to create a day as wonderful as this one.

Katie, Julia, and Sierra sat in the stands that night.

I choked back tears during the national anthem. When I came to the plate for the first time—the first time my wife had seen me in a competitive baseball game—Katie sat in the stands with her hands covering her face and cried.

SIXTEEN

I WOKE UP early on the morning of December 7, 2006, to go deer hunting. Groggy, I dressed quickly and downed a cup of coffee. I grabbed my keys and my phone, and I reflexively checked the screen and saw I had a text message.

From a friend, it read, "JESUS NEVER FAILS." I was told to pass it along to nine other people and I would "get good news that day." It wasn't even 5:00 A.M., but I'm not a big believer in tempting fate, and I'm not a big believer in coincidences, as you might have already gathered. I sent it along to nine other people—what could it hurt?—and didn't give it a whole lot of thought.

When I finished hunting—no bucks, unfortunately— I went to work for my brother. Jason is a firefighter who runs a tree service on his days off, and he needed help with a job that day. I could use the extra money and I enjoyed spending time with my brother, so I was tossing pine limbs through a chipper around 11:00 A.M. when I got a call from a baseball scout friend of mine.

"You didn't hear this from me," he said. "The Cubs just took you in the Rule 5 draft."

I didn't know the particulars of the Rule 5 draft, but my friend told me it was good news. The Devil Rays had left me unprotected off the forty-man roster, which meant that any team in baseball could draft me and send $50,000 to the Devil Rays. Maybe the Devil Rays didn't think I'd get taken, or maybe they thought they'd get lucky and finally get something—anything—for their investment back in 1999.

Whatever the case, my friend the scout finished our conversation by telling me the catch: Whatever team drafted me in the Rule 5 draft had to keep me on the major-league roster throughout the 2007 season or risk losing me back to the Devil Rays. It took a second for me to sort this out in my mind, but when I did, I came up with this summary: If I had a good spring training, chances were I'd be in the big leagues for the entire 2007 season.

In the past four seasons, I'd played very little. Since being reinstated the summer before, I had played fifteen games at Class A Hudson Valley, a far cry from the big leagues. And now, because of some arcane baseball rule, none of that mattered.

I told Jason the news, still not sure how excited I should be. He seemed to know more about it than I did. He shut off the chainsaw and looked at me with big eyes. "That's awesome," he said. "Do you understand what that means?"

Just then, my phone rang again. It was the scout again.

"Check that," he said. "What I told you before was true, but the Cubs just traded you to the Reds. They made a deal before the draft—the Reds wanted you, so the Cubs agreed to draft you first and sell you to the Reds."

The Cubs, the Reds...who really cared? Nothing against the Devil Rays, but there was probably too much history there for me to ever truly break out and succeed. But inside a ballroom at the Walt Disney World Resort in

Orlando, my name had been called twice and my life had taken another unexpected turn.

And this time, miracle of all miracles, the tide seemed to be going my way.

This was the kind of news I was afraid to pray for. This was sent directly from heaven, a phenomenal opportunity. Number-one draft pick or not, I was a twenty-five-year-old man with a history of serious drug problems and less than a hundred at bats above Class A. In the past four years, I had played a total of fifteen games, all at low-level Class A. And now I was being given the opportunity to make a major-league twenty-five-man roster with a productive spring training? Really, all I had to do was show promise and the Reds would most likely keep me around for a while to see what I could do.

I couldn't help but think of the text message I had received that morning. Jesus Never Fails? I guess. Good news? This was ridiculously good news.

My interest in the tree job immediately disappeared. I got a call from Rob Butcher in the Reds' media-relations department, telling me the Cincinnati media wanted to talk to me. We arranged a quick press conference over the phone, and within an hour I was sitting on a tree stump talking to reporters on my cell phone, being asked what it felt like to be a major-league ballplayer.

In the background, Jason stood there waiting for me to finish. With a smile on his face, every so often he'd yell something about needing me to get off the phone and get back to work. Didn't these people understand he had a job to finish here?

It was a pretty cool moment to share with Jason. When he would yell out I'd try not to laugh while holding my hand over the mouthpiece. We'd gone through a lot over the past six or seven years. After being inseparable as kids, we had drifted apart as the drugs took me away from family and friends. He had his life with his two children and his two jobs, and I was the irresponsible one—the prodigal son, even—who squandered everything he was given and still remained the center of attention.

As I sat there talking on the phone and trying not to let Jason make me laugh, I remembered standing on the mound at Tropicana Field two days after the draft, winding up to throw the first pitch and winking at Bro just before I threw it. We hadn't shared many pure moments since then, but this one felt like a beginning of something and the end of something else.

I made it through the press conference, and I have no doubt my disbelief about the entire turn of events came through loud and clear. I still didn't entirely understand what had happened to me, but I walked away from my last tree job knowing I had to get to work to make sure the Reds' confidence in me—or was it more of a hunch, or a calculated risk?—was deserved.

Either way, the Reds showed remarkable confidence in me by giving me a chance to play at the big-league level. The compliment, to me, was directed more toward my recovery than my baseball ability.

It was easy to place a bet on my ability to hit a baseball and track down a fly ball. But based on my personal history, it took serious guts to believe I could stay clean and sober.

Even as I talked to the reporters and expressed my excitement, my confidence was building. I knew that once I got on the field, everything would be just fine. I could play—I could *always* play—and now my mind was as straight as my body.

I remembered what Katie had told me back when I was in the process of wasting my gifts and endangering my life:

God spoke to my soul and told me someday you're going to be back playing baseball. Josh, there's a bigger plan for you. When you come back, it's going to be about more than baseball.

I told her to be quiet back when she said those words. Now, when I got home on the night of the Rule 5 draft, I told her about the text message I had received that morning. Then I hugged her and said, "It looks like you were right all along."

The signs had been there for some time, ever since I sat in Granny's back bedroom, fighting off the cravings with Scripture. This was a God thing. How could it be anything else?

■ ■ ■

Reds general manager Wayne Krivsky called his manager after the Rule 5 draft to tell him the news. Wayne was excited about drafting me and giving me a chance to fulfill all the promise I had misplaced along the way.

And when he told Jerry Narron that he had drafted Josh Hamilton, Narron couldn't believe it. "I've known Josh since he was a kid," Narron said. Krivsky had no idea. He didn't know I played basketball with Johnny Narron's son when I was twelve, or that I'd played for Johnny when I was fifteen, or that Johnny had begged his brother Jerry to come watch me play, promising "You've never seen anything like this kid."

Jerry Narron contacted me, and I got back in touch with Johnny. I started working out even more seriously, intent upon making the most of this chance. I worked out with weights, something I'd done only intermittently in the past. I worked with a medicine ball to increase my bat speed and core strength. Johnny still lived in Raleigh, so he helped me by throwing batting practice and hitting me fly balls.

My recovery was a big topic. It was one thing to play a few games in the minor leagues with my family with me and quite another to face the prospect of an entire major-league season—the travel, the temptations, the down time—so shortly after achieving my sobriety. This was a worry for the Reds, for Katie, and for me. I wanted this opportunity to work out—I wanted that more than I'd ever wanted anything—but I wanted to make sure it was done with my long-term health in mind.

This was part of my new priorities—God, family, and baseball, in that order. And if I took care of the first two, the third would follow naturally.

The more time I spent with Johnny Narron, the more comfortable I felt. Johnny is a fatherly man whose personal values fit well with mine. He is a man of faith who practices what he preaches in a quiet manner. His calm demeanor and laid-back North Carolina temperament allowed us to get along like lifelong friends.

The Reds agreed to give Johnny a job as the team's video coordinator. Mostly, he was hired to be with me. I don't like the term *babysitter* because I don't think it's fair or accurate, but Johnny essentially was hired to play the role my parents had played in my early years in the minors. He was with me, would look after me, and cared about me. I know it was an unusual arrangement for a big-league player, but my situation and circumstances were unusual.

In the event I ended up making the team, Johnny,

Katie, and I made a plan for road trips. At the beginning of every road trip, big-leaguers are given an envelope full of cash to handle meal expenses for the trip. It's nearly eighty dollars a day, and we decided right away that Johnny would take my meal money and dole it out to me as I needed it. He would accompany me to the ballpark and back every day, and he would be available to me if I needed him, whenever or wherever that might be.

Johnny's hiring had the potential to be controversial. However, I looked at Johnny as an insurance policy for the Reds. They were making an investment in my talent, and Johnny was there to help ensure that I got the most of it. None of this was guaranteed, but I set out to prove I was worth the risk.

■ ■ ■

One afternoon a few days before I was to report to spring training in Florida, one of my brother's firefighter friends called me to ask a favor.

"Josh, would you consider talking to my son? He's a good ballplayer and a good kid, but he's made some bad decisions and I'm worried about him."

The boy was flunking out of his senior year in high school. He had moved out of his parents' home and was living with his girlfriend. He was smoking a lot of pot and listening to nobody. He had admired me as a ballplayer in years past, and his dad thought I might be able to reach him.

I agreed to try. Katie and I had done some speaking in local churches on forgiveness and redemption, and I had grown comfortable professing my faith to large groups. We spoke about our relationship to five thousand people at Hope Community Church in Apex. All we had to do was be honest and tell our stories, and let the power of our words and God's mercy carry the day.

This, however, was different. I was a little nervous about a one-on-one with a troubled teenager. I had my story, and he had his. I know from experience that people in trouble are often the last to recognize it, and they don't always listen.

The next day I went to Clayton High School with my Bible in my hand. I went to the office, found what class he was in, and asked them if they'd mind pulling him out of class to talk to me for a few minutes.

He had no idea any of this was planned, as the look on his face showed. I introduced myself—he knew who I was, but still—and then walked with him to the school's baseball field.

"You know your parents are worried about you, right?"

"Yeah, I guess."

"I've made some mistakes. I know how hard it can be, but there's a better way."

He listened but said little. I opened the Bible to a passage I had chosen before leaving home: Romans 7:14–17. I read to him.

For we know that the law is spiritual, but I am unspiritual—sold into slavery to sin. For I do not understand what I am doing. For I do not do what I want—instead, I do what I hate. But if I do what I don't want, I agree that the law is good. But now it is no longer me doing it, but sin that lives in me.

I discussed the meaning of the passage, and how Paul battled with sin. It's the battle that is waged within all of us, the battle between sin and salvation.

"It's never too late," I told him. "Just look at me."

■ ■ ■

Before I left for spring training with the Reds, I had to take care of an important piece of unfinished business. Julia and I made the decision to formally be welcomed into our faith and be baptized together by our pastor, Jimmy Carroll of Journey Church in Raleigh. With a new, unexpectedly wonderful opportunity in front of me, it was the perfect time to give thanks and praise to God.

Our church wasn't completed yet, so there was no baptismal pool. This called for some ingenuity and resourcefulness. Pastor Jimmy arranged for us to be baptized at the Gypsy Divers Aquatic Shop in Raleigh, where we would use one of their diving pools for the ceremony.

The symbolism of baptism as it related to my story made it even more important, and poignant. Being immersed in a pool of God's healing water—even in a dive shop—is just an outward sign of an inward transformation. My inward transformation, while never complete, began the day I was saved in my aunt's living room. It strengthened the day I surrendered to God in the tiny bedroom in my grandmother's house and told Him to do with me what He would. I admitted my inadequacies and acknowledged my inability to overcome my problems on my own.

And now, getting ready to head to a major-league spring training after nearly four years out of the game, I was a living example of God's generosity and power. I was a miracle, and it seemed the absolute perfect time for me to exercise an outward manifestation of my inner transformation. I proclaimed to the Lord, publicly, that I am a follower of Christ. I needed to confirm and celebrate my faith as spring approached and I prepared for the next step of my journey.

I told Katie I didn't expect to feel any different when I emerged from the water. I already felt different inside; I already felt reborn and released from the bonds of my imprisonment. A dip in the pool was just confirmation.

So, with Katie's mother and father watching along with about forty other people from our congregation, I walked fully clothed into the water. When I emerged, the smile on my face could have lit up the night. I looked up to see Katie and her parents with tears streaming down their faces. I really did feel different. My heart felt light. This was a moment of pure happiness.

I stayed in the water and Julia joined me. Katie says the smile that stayed on my face was the biggest she had ever seen. When I walked out of the water with Julia, I felt a lightness and happiness that surprised me.

SEVENTEEN

ON FEBRUARY 15, 2007, I arrived at the Reds' complex in Sarasota and walked into a spring training clubhouse for the first time in four years. The butterflies bounced in my stomach like a thousand jackrabbits. So much of this was unexpected, and now that it was here, and real, I couldn't help but be nervous.

It didn't feel real, though, especially when I looked across the room and saw Ken Griffey Jr.'s, locker. I didn't have any idea how I'd fit in, whether I belonged here either mentally or physically. I had played eight Class A games in the past four years, and I had never played a single inning at a level above Class AA.

What was I doing here? Following the script, I guess.

I didn't know how I was going to be received by the players or the fans or the media. My failures and mistakes were well publicized, so I knew I would come under more scrutiny than anybody else in camp. I knew my story would be a favorite of the national writers and broadcasters who made their trips through the spring training camps, as well as the Cincinnati media.

The reception I would get and the way in which I would be projected through the media were things I could not control. I could be honest and grateful and give glory to God, but once the words left my mouth they were open for interpretation and dissection.

On the field, I had fewer worries. Sixteen months of sobriety and positive thinking had convinced me I hadn't lost my ability to play the game. Somehow, after abusing my body and my brain and my soul for so long, I found I could still play. Once I got my strength and my weight back, I was amazed that I could still throw and run and hit the ball as far as I always could. If this wasn't a miracle, nothing is.

The first batting practice with the Reds dispelled most of my fears. I knew I would be watched closely, by teammates and coaches, and after a few swings I realized I was right with these guys. I could swing it with Jeff Conine and Adam Dunn and the other veteran big-leaguers.

I felt everyone's eyes on me, and that was nothing new. After I sprayed a few balls all over the field, I took a couple out and started to hear the same whispers and see the same head nods I'd grown accustomed to before I left the game. I played it cool, but inside I was smiling. I got a couple of back slaps from my teammates, and I knew I had a chance to make this work.

Before the spring training games began, Jerry Narron called me into his office to tell me I would be playing just about every day during the spring.

"For you to get your timing, and for us to see if you can play up here, you need to play," he said. "Right now I'm looking at moving you around from center to right to designated hitter when we can. I want you to get as many at bats as you can."

This sounded perfect to me. They needed to see it, and so did I. By this time, two weeks into official workouts, I was feeling confident I could stick around. There were some problems—I felt out of place and unsure on the basepaths, like I was on the surface of the moon or something—but I showed I could still play.

I started the Grapefruit League on a tear, hitting a 450-foot homer in my first at bat, and stayed that way. I think my frame of mind—I was incredibly happy and eager to wake up and get to the park every morning—had a lot to do with it. This was the chance I never thought I would get, and making the most of it felt better than any high I could imagine. After praying for the Lord to take me away from the horrible mess of my life, I was now thanking Him and praising Him for every second of every day.

I was routinely asked, "When did you know you were going to be able to play in the big leagues?" About half-way through spring training, when I was hitting nearly .500, I faced Mariano Rivera of the Yankees. Rivera is one of the best relievers in the history of baseball, and you could make a serious argument that he is the very best.

I had never faced Rivera, but I asked some guys in the dugout and they said he throws one pitch—a cut fastball that moves so much it's nearly impossible to hit. It's very rare for a pitcher, even a closer, to rely on one pitch, but Rivera is considered a freak of nature when it comes to this one pitch.

Quickly, I fell behind in the count 1-2. I had seen nothing but the cutter, and I had a couple good rips at it. So, on 1-2, I was looking for another one. The ball left Rivera's hand, and I geared up to get the bat through in time. But when I started to swing, the ball was nowhere near me—a changeup. It's one of the worst feelings in baseball: looking for a fastball and getting fooled by a changeup. I lunged for the ball and missed it badly, striking out and looking silly in the process.

That was a shock. Nobody even knew Mariano Rivera threw a changeup, and here he was, throwing it to a rookie in spring training. Jeff Conine came to the plate and was surprised to see Rivera and catcher Jose Posada looking at each other and laughing. Conine's been around forever and knows everybody, so he asked Posada, "What's so funny?"

"Mo just threw one of the three changeups he'll throw all season."

I took it as a compliment. I was deemed worthy to be the unfortunate recipient of one of Mariano Rivera's select few changeups. I guess that's when I realized I'd made it.

■ ■ ■

Before a spring training game in late March, less than two weeks from Opening Day, I was standing near the dugout signing autographs. I never looked at this as a chore, even back in high school, because if someone thinks enough of you to spend the money to watch you play and ask you for an autograph, it's the least we can do to sign a piece of paper or a baseball cap.

I was going from baseball card to cap to program, signing as fast as I could, when I heard a voice that sounded vaguely familiar. With everybody calling out your name, it's usually best to keep your head down and sign, but something about this man's voice made me look up.

What I saw startled me. It was Kevin from the tattoo shop, the man who had introduced me to drugs. He was with his son, by now about eight, and they were handing me something to sign.

I had thought about what might happen if I ever saw these guys again. For years I felt resentment and bitterness toward them, even though I knew I made my own decisions and was responsible for the consequences.

"Hi, Josh," Kevin said. "Good to see you're doing well."

I held eye contact, unsmiling, for a little longer than usual. I had a brief flashback to all the years of hell that started with one bad decision.

I nodded to the boy, whom I assumed was his son even though he'd never mentioned children. Turning back to the cards and baseballs held out before me, I said, "Thanks, man. Hope you're doing well."

I had to remind myself of my standard answer when someone mentioned the guys who got me started in all this: They weren't bad people, they just did bad things.

Forgiveness was at the root of my story. I was forgiven, therefore I needed to forgive. I knew there would be more encounters with fans who, for whatever reason, felt the need to belittle me because of my past, but looking up to see Kevin was a moment that might not be topped.

Before spring training began, I had no idea how I would be received by fans. I knew other players who had drug problems, like Darryl Strawberry, became targets of fan abuse. I didn't know what to expect, and I definitely didn't expect what I got.

From the beginning, I was reminded every day that my story is bigger than me. Every time I go to the ballpark, I talk to people who are either battling addictions themselves or trying to help someone else who is. They want to confide in me, to share, to see if something I experienced can help them succeed as well.

Who talks to me? Just about everybody.

A father will tell me about his son while I'm signing autographs. A mother will wait outside the players' parking lot to tell me about her daughter. They know where

I've been. They remind me that this isn't really about baseball.

A man called to me during spring training and told me his son was a meth addict who loved baseball. A story about me in *USA Today* had caught the father's attention, and he gave it to his son and told him to read it. When he finished, his son said, "I'm going to give it a try. If he can do it, so can I."

It had been two weeks since his son read the article, the father said, but it had been a good two weeks. His smile could have lit up the ballpark, and the tears in his eyes caused me to reach up over the railing and pat him on the back.

"Tell your son I said, 'Stay strong,'" I told him.

■ ■ ■

It became official the weekend before Opening Day: I made the team as the fourth outfielder. I wouldn't say it was anticlimactic, but it didn't carry the same power and emotion as the day Andrew Friedman called to tell me I'd been reinstated. The truth was, I hit .403 during spring training and was one of the feel-good stories in baseball. Everybody, including me, might have been surprised that I found myself in this position, but after six weeks of spring training nobody was surprised I broke camp as a major-league ballplayer.

As we flew to Cincinnati for the opener against the Cubs, though, I had some time to think about these five words:

Josh Hamilton, major-league ballplayer.

It sounds both completely natural and utterly unbelievable. To the folks back home in Raleigh, who saw me play from the time I was six, this was predestined, a simple result of the world's natural order. *Josh Hamilton, major-league ballplayer?* There was never any question in the minds of the parents who feared for their children's safety, or in the minds of the scouts who watched me at Athens Drive High School, or in the minds of my minor-league teammates with the Princeton Devil Rays or the Charleston RiverDogs.

But ask the people who populated my other life and they'll tell you *Josh Hamilton, major-league ballplayer* must be some kind of mistake.

The doctors in the emergency rooms who counted my heartbeat through my shirt as they treated me after I ingested near-overdose levels of cocaine—they'll tell you the idea of this man someday performing at the highest level of his sport never occurred to them. They were simply trying to save my life before shrugging and telling my parents there was really nothing they could do if their son was determined to kill himself.

And the guys who lived and sold crack out of the trailer. Ask them what they think of the words *Josh Hamilton, major-league ballplayer* and they'll probably laugh right in your face, tell you to get that shit out of here, man.

■ ■ ■

With Opening Day the next afternoon, there was very little sleep to be found on the night of April 1, 2007. My mind raced all night, thinking about the twisted, rutted road I'd traveled to this point. I thought this night— the night before my first big-league game—would happen much sooner. Then I thought it would never happen at all.

It felt like I broke everything in my path and then somehow managed to put it all back together. The people who had been with me, my parents and Katie and her parents and my brother and Granny, were still here. They left, and then they came back.

Just like me.

EIGHTEEN

ON THE MORNING of April 2, 2007, Opening Day, Katie and I woke up in our rented condo outside Cincinnati and went about our business as if we couldn't believe this day had come. To the girls, it was just another day of watching Daddy play baseball, but for us it was almost surreal. In a matter of hours, I would be jogging from the home dugout to the first-base line in a Cincinnati Reds uniform as the public-address announcer introduced me to more than forty-two thousand people.

I didn't know how the fans would react to me, but I knew I had my own cheering section. My parents, Katie's parents, Julia and Sierra, Steve Reed—all of them were there, sitting near the Reds' dugout. I wanted Granny to be there, but her health didn't allow her to travel. She was home watching it on television. (She bought the "Extra Innings" package the second she found out I made the team.)

My parents got to the ballpark as early as possible, just like old times.

I arrived more than four hours before game time. There was a locker with my name over it, so I wasn't dreaming this. The minutes seemed like hours as I tried to stay busy and tried not to watch the clock. I got more nervous and more excited with every passing minute.

This was really happening.

There's not a lot of serious talk during times like this. The clubhouse is a place for bluster and wisecracks more than deep thoughts, but I could feel the eyes on me occasionally as everybody went about their business. This was a big day for everybody, but it was an unreal day for me. I sensed that many of my teammates understood that.

Jeff Conine walked up to me as I was sitting in front of my locker. This was Jeff's seventeenth Opening Day, and the Reds were his sixth team over those seventeen years. He'd seen just about all there was to see in the big leagues, which made him one of the guys I respected most on the team.

Jeff looked down at me with a knowing smile on his face.

"You excited?"

"Oh, yeah," I said. "Oh, yeah."

Jeff broke into the big leagues with the Kansas City Royals in 1990, on a team with Bo Jackson and George Brett. He told me he remembered when he was in my position, fidgeting and waiting for his first big-league game. Brett and Jackson both took the time to speak to him, and he felt their words were worth repeating in this situation.

"Just remember this: Between the lines, it's just baseball," he said. "No matter the level, it's the same game you've been playing your whole life. Everything else is different once you get up here, but they didn't change the game. If you can keep that straight, you'll be fine."

I made the team as the fourth outfielder, and I wasn't in the lineup on Opening Day. During batting practice I watched the stands fill and my family gather in their seats near the Reds' dugout. It didn't take long for me to discover how I would be received by the hometown fans. The fans in Cincinnati love baseball and love the Reds, and from the moment the fans entered the stadium I was greeted with cheers and autograph requests from everyone from elderly women to little boys in their Reds caps.

I had to prepare myself for the pregame introductions, because I knew it was going to be difficult to keep a lid on my emotions. They introduced the nonstarters first, and as it got closer to my turn I could feel my heart beating faster and faster. When I reached the steps of the dugout, waiting for my name to be called, I had to swallow hard to keep from crying tears of joy. By that point, I didn't want to try to speak. I don't think it would have worked.

And when they introduced me—"No. 33, outfielder Josh Hamilton"—I jogged to the third-base line. I tried to be cool, but the noise blew me away. By the time I finished shaking hands with my teammates and faced the crowd, everybody was standing. The cheers came down on me like a waterfall, and I stood there with a big silly grin on my face.

I looked up into the stands, at the people who stayed by my side, and I nodded my appreciation. Katie and my parents and her parents were all crying. I saw Sierra and Julia, and the looks on their faces made me proud. On the outside, I looked like I was together. I plastered a smile on my face and felt the burning in my throat as I held back the tears. I was a big-leaguer, and I had to act like one. Inside, though, was a different story: Deep down, I was a big puddle.

There was just no way to express the gratitude I felt as I took the field that day. Everywhere I looked I saw a reminder of God's glory. The fans in the stands, with their big-hearted acceptance of me. My family, with their loyalty and forgiveness. Myself, with the gifts He wouldn't allow me to squander, no matter how hard I tried.

It was here. About four years late, at the end of a windy, rocky road, I made it. And at that moment, despite everything that had happened to me, I wouldn't have traded it for anything in the world. I wouldn't have traded it for four more years in the big leagues or a few million more dollars or anything else you could think of.

Everything that had happened was leading to this moment. It couldn't have happened any other way.

■ ■ ■

In the bottom of the eighth inning, Jerry Narron told me to get ready to pinch-hit. I bounced over to the bat rack and felt my heartbeat quicken and the butterflies start a riot in my stomach.

Our pitcher, Kirk Saarloos, was coming up that inning, and Narron called on me to bat for him. I walked to the on-deck circle on a cloud, trying and failing to think about what I needed to do when I got into the batter's box.

As I left the dugout, the cheering started and didn't stop. I looked around, trying to be nonchalant, and was shocked to see some of the fans start to stand. Then more stood, and more.

It felt like an electrical current was running through my body. I couldn't believe what I was seeing, and the noise level made the pregame introduction sound like someone whispering in church.

Nearly everyone was standing when Cubs manager Lou Piniella—the man who had listened to my lies three years ago and patiently told me to get my life straight—started out of the dugout to make a pitching change. He removed right-hander Michael Wuertz and called for lefty Will Ohman.

I stood in the on-deck circle and wondered if this was really me. I was swinging a bat and loosening up, but my mind was far away. This was the moment nobody thought would ever arrive, and I looked around and thanked God for the opportunity. Nothing could compare to this moment, ever, and I realized this was the way things had to be. No bemoaning the mistakes I'd made or the years I'd lost. This was reality. This was fate. This was the way God meant for it to be, and I was merely His instrument.

The noise died some as Ohman took his warmup pitches, but it picked up again when I was announced. By the time I got into the batter's box, it was deafening. I smiled and looked around in amazement, nearly forgetting why I was there.

I couldn't see them, but everyone in my family was crying. As I dug into the batter's box and took a couple of practice swings, trying to calm my heart and my nerves, they kept standing and cheering.

Cubs catcher Michael Barrett, crouching behind the plate, looked up at me through the bars of his mask and said, "You deserve it, Josh. Take it all in, brother. I'm happy for you."

Now, the hard part. The crowd's noise died down and the work began. I was so excited and my mind was so scattered I didn't think there was a chance I was going to have much of an at bat.

But then Ohman threw, and I hit the ball. I wanted to jump up and down and throw my hands into the air. I was so pumped up, so filled with emotion, that I surprised myself by even being able to see the ball, let alone make contact and hit it pretty hard. I watched the ball fly over the shortstop's head toward the left fielder, and I thought I had a flare single.

That might have happened in the movie version, but in real life—and in the big leagues—the ball was caught by Cubs' left fielder, Matt Murton, who ran in a long way and made a rolling catch at his ankles.

I jogged back to the dugout, and the cheering started again. The people stood again, more than forty-two thousand of them. This was the third standing ovation I received in about ten minutes, and I was once again amazed at the outpouring of support. When I reached the dugout, several of my teammates greeted me. Ken Griffey Jr., gave me a playful one-armed hug around the neck. How cool is that?

■ ■ ■

I am an addict. That didn't change when I made it to the big leagues. And because I am an addict, I have to go about my business differently. When we're at home, the variables are a little easier to control, especially when Katie and the girls are with me. On the road, however, with so much idle time in new cities, I needed a plan to keep myself focused.

Johnny handled my meal money, and he was always there for me at any hour of the day. We traveled to and from the ballparks together, whether it was walking or by taxi. We ate most meals and often did our daily devotionals together. He was an insurance policy for the team, as well as someone who could run interference for me if something came up that I didn't know how to handle.

Being a rookie is difficult enough, but being a different kind of rookie made it that much harder. I am not a confrontational person by nature, and rookies are supposed to be subservient in the baseball culture, but there were times when the baseball culture and my well-being came into conflict.

For one thing, there's a certain amount of rookie hazing that goes on in the big leagues. Rookie relief pitchers have to carry a bag with sunflower seeds and chewing tobacco and other staples for the guys in the bullpen. Often that bag is as embarrassing as possible—a pink Barbie backpack or something along those lines.

Most of the traditions are meant to be in good fun, and I played along just fine. But one rookie duty is to carry the beer on road trips. Alcohol is a big part of the culture in baseball, although recent events—especially the tragedy of pitcher Josh Hancock's death in St. Louis—have forced baseball to take a closer look at the intelligence of letting players use the clubhouse as a bar after games.

With the Reds, one of the rookies' jobs was to carry a bag of beer from the clubhouse to the bus when we left on a road trip, and then to carry it from the bus to the charter plane once we reached the airport.

I didn't have a moral objection; everyone's an adult and whoever wants to drink a beer on the plane should be able to do it. But before the first road trip of my rookie season, I declined when I was asked—or, rather, told—to carry the beer by one of the veterans.

When I unexpectedly found myself in the big leagues, one of my main goals was to be one of the guys. I wanted to fit in, to laugh and joke and hang out with my teammates the way I did in high school and in my first two years in the minors. But situations arose that pointed out an important fact: I was different. Part of my sobriety is to acknowledge the situations where I *have* to be different, and not let myself be drawn into uncomfortable positions just to fit in.

Carrying a bag of beer from the clubhouse to the bus might seem like a minor concession for me to make, but it didn't feel right. I told my teammate I couldn't do it. I told him I wasn't making any judgment about guys having a few beers on a plane flight, but I didn't think it would be a good idea for me to be seen carrying a bag of beer onto a bus or a plane.

"How is it going to look if somebody takes a picture of me while I'm carrying a bag of beer," I said. "I really don't want to risk that."

He was cool about it. Everyone seemed to understand, and I wasn't asked to do it again. I'm sensitive about how I'm viewed, and that incident was a reminder that I am a little different, that there are limits to how much I can be "one of the boys."

Beyond that, my first road trip caused me some trepidation. Mostly, it was another trip into the unknown. I knew the reception from visiting fans wouldn't be as friendly and welcoming as it was in Cincinnati, and I thought and prayed long and hard for the strength and the wisdom to be able to handle myself in the right way. In the end, I decided I had to be myself, to continue to be honest and forthright with everyone, to own up to my mistakes and allow people to make their own judgments.

In St. Louis, I stood in the outfield at Busch Stadium between innings, playing catch with the left fielder. I expected heckling in the visiting ballparks, and I wasn't disappointed. There was one guy in the bleachers who was really giving it to me, and for his big finish he yelled, "My name is Josh Hamilton and I'm a drug addict."

I smiled a little and looked up at him. I spread my arms out wide and raised my palms to the sky.

"Tell me something I don't know," I said.

Immediately, the fans around him started cheering and laughing. The guy seemed stunned initially, probably shocked and maybe embarrassed that I had called his bluff, but then he recovered and said, "Dude, you're my new favorite player."

I learned how to handle the hecklers, and they weren't all as easy as that guy in St. Louis. I heard everything, from chants of "crackhead" to people telling me to snort the foul lines. From the tone of their voices and the harshness—or playfulness—of their words, I learned which hecklers I could play around with and which I needed to ignore.

My theory was simple: Most of the people with the anger and viciousness in their voices were the ones who had been hurt the most by addiction. I didn't take it personally. I knew they weren't angry at me but at the helplessness and sorrow that comes from being trapped in a situation they perceive as being hopeless. They lashed out at me because they had a brother or a mother or a friend who couldn't escape addiction. Maybe they were the ones who were struggling, and seeing me on the baseball field having a good time, free of my personal torture, hurt them in some way that caused them to direct their anger at me.

It's not something I can easily describe, but I could always tell when someone unleashing a stream of nastiness from the stands was using me to shield themselves from their own pain. I knew I couldn't turn and address those people the way I did the guy in St. Louis, but their words and the venom behind them sent chills down my spine.

As I said every chance I got, nobody can say or do

anything to me that comes close to the damage I did to myself. I believe I can handle the anger from the people who feel the need to use words to bring me down, but I wonder: Can they?

■ ■ ■

On the field, the adjustment to the big-league level was smoother than I had anticipated. There were problems—my baserunning wasn't up to my standards, and I could look foolish on good offspeed pitches—but there were moments when I felt like I did in high school, when my natural ability and instincts took over.

My first hit and first home run came on the same pitch, from Edgar Gonzalez of the Arizona Diamondbacks on our first road trip. I hit two home runs in a game against the Colorado Rockies. Before word spread about my arm, teams tested me and I responded by throwing out runners at third and at the plate. Even though this was trial by fire, I started well enough to be named the National League Rookie of the Month for April.

My favorite baseball moment—better than a home run—comes when I find myself camping under a fly ball in center field and a runner at third is tagging up to try to score. This moment is the best, filled with anticipation and excitement. As I wait for the ball to settle into my glove, my body slightly behind the ball as I prepare to catch it as my body heads toward home plate, I envision the throw lasering over the infield about six feet off the ground and hitting the catcher's mitt a split-second before the runner begins his slide.

Against Cleveland, that scenario played out perfectly and I threw out a runner at the plate to complete a double play. That, combined with a throw I made to third base on another fly ball to get the Rockies' Willy Taveras—one of the fastest players in the game—made teams stop challenging my arm. I appreciated the compliment, but I missed the excitement.

This was on-the-job training. Before every game, I would ask about that day's pitcher; given my bizarre path to the big leagues, there was little chance I had ever faced him at any level. I usually asked two simple questions: 1) What does he throw? and 2) How fast is his fastball?

Armed with the answers to those two questions, I thought I could go up to the plate with enough knowledge to be able to react to speed and movement. I wouldn't be looking for a curve from a guy who only throws a slider, and I wouldn't be surprised by a 95 mph fastball. Part of hitting for me is making up my own mind and not being overly concerned about what a certain pitcher throws. I've learned to study pitchers more, and to use the ridiculous amount of resources available to me at the big-league level, but I usually find that if I've got my mind and body right at the plate, I'm going to be able to hit whatever comes my way.

The trick to the game, of course, is getting the mind and body right on a consistent basis. This was the biggest adjustment I had to make after not playing baseball regularly for nearly four years. The everyday grind of the big-league season wore on me a little bit, partly because I had played so many games during spring training. There were times when I felt the toll of the years of abusing my body. I was quicker to tire and more susceptible to colds and other infections.

The doctors told me I had done damage to my immune system, damage they couldn't adequately assess at this point. My system was compromised by all those years of attacking it with corrosive drugs and alcohol. I abused my body for years, and I don't know how I kept from destroying it completely. Some lingering effects were to be expected, whether I liked it or not.

So in late May I woke up violently ill in a Cleveland hotel room. I was throwing up repeatedly and felt so weak I had to work hard to get to the phone and call Johnny to get me some help.

Johnny came straight to my room, took one look at me, and said, "I think we might need an ambulance." He called the trainer and he agreed. They got me out of the hotel and into a Cleveland hospital, where they diagnosed me as having gastroenteritis.

I knew what everybody was thinking: *Uh-oh, did Josh relapse?*

It was normal to wonder, especially for those people who didn't know I was drug-tested three times a week, home and away, and would be tossed out of baseball the second a test turned up dirty.

But it was inevitable that a late-night/early-morning trip by ambulance to the hospital would stir up rumors and assumptions. I understand that, and I expect that. My past invites that.

I was released from the hospital the next day, after I'd been filled with enough IV fluids to combat the dehydration. From there, Johnny drove me back to Cincinnati. On the way, he was on the phone constantly with everyone in my family, all of them wondering what happened to me. They didn't ask directly, but I knew what they were really asking: Should we prepare ourselves for another letdown?

Johnny assured them I was sick—just sick and not drug-sick or hangover-sick or any other kind of sick. Just pretty darned sick.

By the second day after I got sick, about the time I started feeling better, the Reds had decided to place me on the fifteen-day disabled list. Since this condition usually lasts two or three days, it was unusual for someone to be placed on the disabled list because of it. True, I understand that I am prone to get worse bouts of common bugs and have them last longer. Still, I was sensitive to the perceptions of others and wondered if this would fuel more speculation.

It did, and some of it came from the team's broadcasters, who wondered aloud on the air whether there was something more going on with me. I felt frustrated by this, since the team could have gotten out in front of it and made it clear that the testing plan—three times a week—provided all the answers anybody needed.

Mostly, I just wanted to play. The Reds weren't picked to be much of a factor in the National League Central, mainly because the bullpen was suspect, but I wanted to be on the field to help the team. The team said the decision to place me on the disabled list was to allow me to recharge my battery, since I had played an unusually large number of innings in spring training after being idle for so many years. That was legitimate, and I accepted that. Had it come earlier it might have kept all the speculation from getting started.

Instead, I was sent to Triple A Louisville to rehab. One of the trips we made was to Durham to play the Devil Rays' Triple A affiliate. This was a homecoming for me, and the Raleigh paper trumpeted my return. I didn't really want to be on a rehab assignment, but this trip was worthwhile.

Before the game, as I was walking toward the dugout, I saw the firefighter friend of my brother's. He was with his son, the boy I had pulled out of class and taken to the baseball field to talk a little bit about decisions and temptations.

His dad shook my hand first, then the boy. They thanked me for taking the time to talk to him. The boy had graduated from high school and was now playing junior-college baseball. He looked good, and his dad said he was doing well.

When we left, I could tell the boy wanted to say something but was a little tongue-tied. I loitered for a second or two to let him collect his thoughts.

"Thanks, Josh," he said. "Thanks for helping me see another side."

■ ■ ■

The encouragement I had received from Michael Barrett before that first at bat became a theme. I was overwhelmed by the number of players and umpires and other baseball people who knew my story and took the time to offer me their support.

As Katie said, way back when it wasn't fashionable to say it, this would be bigger than baseball.

In a game in mid-May, I was walking to the plate to lead off an inning when the catcher jogged to the mound to have a word with his pitcher. As they were talking, the home-plate umpire, whom I will not name, walked around to brush off home plate.

I was smoothing the dirt in the batter's box with my feet, and I could see the plate didn't need to be cleaned. The umpire bent over with his brush in his hand and looked up at me.

"Josh, I'm really pulling for you," he said. "I've fought some battles myself, and I just want you to know I'm rooting for you."

My comeback had blurred so many lines and brought together so many different people, and now it had broken through the sacred separation between umpires and players. Obviously, we talk and joke and argue with umpires, but rarely does an umpire admit to openly rooting for a ballplayer.

In another setting, I would have shaken the man's hand and told him to be strong. In this setting, however, that probably wouldn't have been a good idea.

I nodded and thanked him instead.

Another time I hit a double against the Houston Astros, and as I was standing at the bag waiting for the next hitter, Astros second baseman Craig Biggio came over to talk.

"I'm proud of you, man," he said. "I understand what you're going through. Stay strong. I wish I could have done more for Cammie, but nobody could change him. I just want you to know I'm rooting for you."

"Cammie" was Ken Caminiti, Biggio's former teammate with the Astros and the National League MVP with the Padres in 1996. Caminiti battled the same demons as me, but he couldn't overcome them. He left baseball after the 2001 season and died in New York City on October 10, 2004, of a heart attack caused by an overdose of cocaine and opiates.

That could have been me. I know that, and Biggio knew that. When Caminiti died, everyone wondered how he could have allowed himself to reach the position where he died in a grimy section of the Bronx, hanging out with crackheads and other dead-end people.

People in so-called polite society looked at the money and fame he accumulated as a ballplayer and couldn't understand how he could lose it all. His problems were well documented—he went to rehab for alcohol and admitted cocaine and steroid use—but still there was a collective shock at the way he died.

From the outside, it appeared Caminiti had everything. How could he end up the way he did, and where he did? Easy—he had an addiction that took control of his life. What happened to Ken Caminiti could easily have happened to me. Addiction took away huge chunks of his life—wife, children, baseball—and left him with nothing but a jones for the next high. Addiction is a tornado, clearing everything in its path.

I understand what happened to Caminiti, because it happened to me. Nobody could understand how I could end up hanging out in a trailer park outside Raleigh with a bunch of people who never had anything and made their way through life by taking advantage of people and helping them ruin their lives.

But hey—that's where I was, the $4 million man who was considered the best high school baseball player ever. The first position player drafted number one out of high school since Alex Rodriguez. The next Mickey Mantle. But none of that could stop me from wanting, needing, and getting drugs.

The only thing that stopped me was turning my life over to the Lord and realizing I was no longer in control of my destiny. Once I surrendered, I was able to see the world more clearly and gradually resume living. Sadly, Ken Caminiti never got that chance.

■ ■ ■

My excitement over being in the big leagues was tempered by our team's performance. Our pitching, especially the bullpen, went through some terrible stretches. By mid-June, we were way down in the standings and the inevitable happened: Everyone started talking about whether Jerry Narron's job was on the line.

Everyone expected more out of us. We had a lineup with Adam Dunn, Brandon Phillips, Ken Griffey Jr., and Edwin Encarnacion. We had one of the best starting pitchers in baseball in Aaron Harang. Griffey was counting down to six hundred homers, adding excitement to our games. Despite being a flawed team—bullpen, starting pitching depth—we were expected to be closer to the top of the standings than the bottom.

I became an unwitting part of the discussion regarding the manager's job status. Since Johnny was Jerry's brother, and since he was on the staff because of me, Johnny and I were in the middle of the speculation. Would the Reds fire Jerry and keep Johnny? Would Johnny want to stay employed by a team that fired his brother? And if Johnny left, what would happen to me?

We hit the All-Star break with a record of 31–51 and Jerry was fired. I think he was the scapegoat for our poor performance, but that's been the story of the major-league manager since they invented the position. They don't play, but they're held responsible for how we play.

In the aftermath of Jerry's firing, our second baseman, Brandon Phillips, made some comments that created an uproar in Cincinnati. Asked to comment, Phillips said, "We had a good year with Jerry last year [2006], but we had new guys come to the scene this year. He tried to adjust with the new players this year, but it was all about certain players. Ken Griffey and his home-run chase, Josh Hamilton and his comeback season, everybody got caught up in that instead of winning."

I knew there was some resentment about me, and

Johnny, but this was the first time it had been expressed publicly. Some players evidently felt I was getting special treatment. It was true; not everybody had a special-assignment coach who occupied an adjacent room on road trips and lived in his apartment whenever his family wasn't around. I got it, but I also went out of my way to make sure I didn't flaunt the arrangement or keep Johnny from helping someone else.

I was also conscious of the media attention I was receiving. The volume of requests made it necessary for me to hold a mini–press conference before the first game of every road series. With the help of the Reds' media-relations staff, it was always smooth and low-stress. I made sure I didn't inconvenience my teammates by holding big sessions in the clubhouse, where my teammates would have to tiptoe around a clump of reporters. We held the interviews in the dugout or a separate interview room. The people pay our salaries, and the people were interested in my story, so I looked upon it as part of my job.

There's another important factor: The media helps keep me honest. Whenever I say this to reporters, they always laugh a little and look away, like I'm trying to manipulate them or suck up. That's not what I'm doing. The truth is, speaking to the media helps remind me of the bigger picture—why I'm here, what my mission is, the platform I've been provided by God.

It's a version of therapy for me, answering questions honestly and openly. I know I'm being watched. I know I'm being held to a higher standard because of my past. I accept that. I welcome that. If I did something I shouldn't be doing, everyone would know about it almost immediately. I'd be a hypocrite, and all the work I've done to repair my soul would be wasted.

So I read Phillips's comments and decided to let it slide. I didn't confront him or even discuss it with him. I understood the frustration, even if I didn't understand the resentment. I realized I'd been through worse, and I had a job to do regardless of what they thought. I continued to spend time with the fans, and I didn't turn down interviews if people wanted to know about my story. I just went on with my business and let the other stuff slide.

And when the discussion drifted to Johnny's status, I made it clear that I needed him. At this point in my career, just half a season into my first year as a big-leaguer and less than two years into sobriety, I needed Johnny. In addition, Katie needed Johnny for the peace of mind it gave her when she couldn't be with me.

I had to look out for myself. I am motivated by making good decisions and becoming a better man. It's also why my life is God, family, and baseball. I go from the ballpark to home to the ballpark to home.

Pretty boring, maybe, but I've grown accustomed to boring. In fact, I kind of like it. For me, boring works.

NINETEEN

BASEBALL HAS ALWAYS had an uneasy relationship with Christianity. The old-school, tough-guy mentality of the game has sometimes been at odds with the growing number of players who are open about their faith. It shouldn't be a factor, but some people believe players who make it a point to speak out about their faith are somehow less competitive, or less concerned about wins and losses.

I was created to have an intimate relationship with God and to spread the word. The illogic of my life can be explained only through God—it's a God thing, remember?—and I believe I have an obligation to be open about my faith and the ways in which it delivered me out of darkness.

My obligation is to speak to people who need help, and to spread the word to those who find themselves in situations that seem hopeless. Nobody was more hopeless than me, nobody more aimless or tortured or imprisoned by his own bad choices. Through the mercy and grace of God, I made it out of my own terrible darkness and into this bright and beautiful light. It would be irresponsible and arrogant of me to keep that to myself.

However, I understand there is a fine line between testifying for the Lord and proselytizing. I am open about my faith when I am asked, but I try not to force my beliefs on anybody. During the season, we had chapel every Sunday morning at ten. In a very nonthreatening way, I walked through the Reds' clubhouse and tapped my teammates on the shoulder and said, "Chapel in ten minutes." I moved on, leaving it at that.

It was usually the same people in chapel every Sunday, but one morning about six weeks into the season I turned around during chapel and saw a first-time attendee. It was a teammate I had tapped on the shoulder every Sunday and never expected to see inside the room. He was sitting in the back, by himself, listening. I smiled inside but said nothing.

Small victories.

■　■　■

I'm drug-tested three times a week. I don't expect that to change any time soon. During the season, wherever I am, testers from the company show up and test me on those same three days. They show up at the ballpark or at my in-season home, their kits at the ready.

When I returned to North Carolina after my rookie season, my buddy Dale from the company contracted by Major League Baseball brought his kit to my house, watched me pee, and then marked and sealed the samples to be tested later. Katie and I joked that Dale was part of the family; Sierra and Julia greeted him by name every time he arrived, and he asked them about school and their friends. Dale showed up every Monday, Wednesday, and Friday, no matter where I was. If I was at my in-laws' house, I called Dale and he showed up there. If I was at my parents' house, I called Dale and he met me there.

I know it might seem like an intrusion, maybe even an invasion of privacy, but I welcome it. The testing is mandatory, of course—a missed test is the same as a failed test. I find no shame in the process. In fact, the ritual is liberating to me. I have nothing to hide, and I couldn't hide it if I wanted to. It keeps me honest and allows me to answer every question. Hey, I'm an open book—you don't have to ask me if I'm clean, because the testing makes it obvious. They know what's in my body.

It's the ultimate defense—three days a week they test for everything: narcotics, alcohol, steroids. They send each result to Major League Baseball and the Major League Baseball Players Association. If a test came up dirty, within minutes the news would be running across the crawl at the bottom of an ESPN screen near you.

As time passed during my rookie season, I thought about using less and less. The feeling I got waking up every morning with a clear head and a clear conscience was winning the battle. There were still remnants of the bad old days, however—mostly at night. One night after a game in St. Louis, Johnny and I were walking back from the ballpark to the hotel. I was quiet but agitated, and Johnny could tell right away something wasn't right.

"Something wrong, Josh?" he asked.

I had been having thoughts about using again, thoughts sparked by a series of dreams I'd had. In the dreams, I would be putting all the stuff together—the rosebud vase, the Chore Boy, the crack. It was so real I even started to smell it in my dreams. I'd get right to the point where I'd be ready to put the pipe to my mouth and I'd stop. Sometimes I'd look to the side and see the pee-test guy standing there. At this point, I'd always wake up, always before I made the decision to use.

I didn't tell Johnny about the dreams at that moment, but I said, "I need to do a devotional."

Johnny didn't ask why. We went to his room and discussed what was on our minds, then we read from Scripture. I don't remember exactly what passage we discussed that night, but it was exactly what I needed at the time.

Another time, in Philadelphia, Johnny's wife, Gail, was on the trip. It was past midnight after a game, and I was restless. I had thoughts about going out, and even though I knew I wasn't going to act on them I needed some reassurance. I called Johnny, reluctantly, and asked him if they wanted to get something to eat.

He knew food had nothing to do with it, of course, and within a few minutes the three of us were sitting in a booth at a Wendy's in downtown Philadelphia. We didn't stay long, but the restlessness left me and I slept soundly.

■ ■ ■

By all accounts, my rookie year with the Reds was a success. I hit .292 with 19 homers. My low RBI total—47— was mostly a result of hitting leadoff most of the season. I was thrilled to be back in the game and especially thrilled—and stunned—to be in the major leagues, but I knew I had just scratched the surface of my potential.

At some point during the season, each of the papers in the Tampa area sent someone out to talk to me about my success and the wild turns of events in my life. In one of them, Devil Rays' GM Andrew Friedman—the man who had been on the other end of the best phone call of my life—said I would have started the season in Class A if I had remained with Tampa Bay. I give Andrew high marks for honesty, but to me that was yet another indication that everything in my life was happening for a reason that nobody could adequately explain.

■ ■ ■

I developed a reputation around the league as someone who was fun to watch during batting practice. As I had in my days in the minor leagues, I enjoyed watching other players' reactions when I took batting practice. Early in the season before a game in Cincinnati against the Braves I was hitting rockets all over the place, and the Braves were looking up from their stretching. It went from one guy to the next, and pretty soon they were all watching.

On my last swing, I hit one onto the fake riverboat behind center field at Great American Ballpark. It was a bomb, probably five hundred feet, and I heard a couple of the Braves as they were walking out of the cage saying, "Did you see where he hit that ball?"

Still, my expectations for the season were higher. For one, I was disappointed in how we played as a team, finishing 72–90, ahead of only the Pirates in the NL Central. For another, I was disappointed that I played in just ninety games. I went into the off-season determined to get myself in shape to make it through an entire 162-game season.

I wanted to get rid of the nagging stuff that cost me so many games—sixteen games with gastroenteritis, twenty-nine games with a sprained right wrist, and the last seventeen games of the year with a hamstring strain.

During the off-season, I started hearing the first faint whispers of trade rumor. The Reds needed to revamp their team, and they took the first step by hiring Dusty Baker to replace interim manager Pete Mackanin. The next item on their agenda was to improve their pitching, which really dragged down the team.

The Reds needed a young, quality starting pitcher. The Reds had too many good outfielders. Naturally, they identified the teams that had a need in the outfield, and they quickly settled on the Rangers, a team that needed a center fielder and had a few good arms in the minors the Reds liked.

In baseball, very little happens by accident. Trades and free-agent signings are researched and re-researched, and as soon as it became known the Reds might be interested in trading me, the Rangers went to work. They sent scouts to watch me speak to church groups. They talked to drug counselors and psychologists and anybody else who could shed light on addiction and recovery. They liked what they heard. General manager Jon Daniels kept hearing the same reports: Addicts who rely on faith-based recovery have far better success rates than those who don't.

I didn't give much thought to the trade talk. Instead, I was intent on getting my body in the kind of shape that would last for 162 games. Instead of doing a lot of baseball work, I went to Pilates three or four times a week and worked out with college football players from North Carolina State and the University of North Carolina who were preparing for the draft at a training center in Raleigh. I rocked my weight up to about 245 and got both stronger and faster.

I had never been timed in the forty-yard dash, and I clocked a 4.5. I had never had my vertical leap measured, and it was thirty-two. I no longer felt I was making up for lost time. This time around, instead of pushing myself to get ready for my last best chance, I was laying a foundation for a career.

And then, on December 21, 2007, I got a call informing me the Reds had traded me to the Rangers for minor-
league pitchers Edinson Volquez and Danny Herrera.
Volquez was the prime target of the Reds, and right away
the Rangers committed to playing me in center field
every day.

■ ■ ■

In a big-league clubhouse, every player has a mailbox on
the wall. It's a big grid, with each box about four inches by
six inches, open at the end. After a week in Surprise, Arizona, spring training home of the Texas Rangers, I was
confused. There were two letters in my slot. I'm not trying to brag, but I wasn't used to having just two letters in
my slot.

In Cincinnati, I couldn't keep up with the letters. I
read most of them and then had them sent to my parents'
house in North Carolina, where my momma read them
and organized them for me to respond. Many of them
were just people seeking autographs, but a good number of
the letters I received were heartfelt, passionate notes from
people who either appreciated my story or were seeking
help with their own or a loved one's addiction problems. I
liked to read them, especially when I was in a contempla-
tive mood, to remind myself how many people I've been
able to reach with my story.

It always made me feel good to open up a letter from
someone who drew inspiration from my recovery. If things
weren't going well for me at the plate I'd often open a few
letters and remember what is really important, and why
I believe I was serving a higher calling by regaining my
ability and desire to play baseball. But anyway, after two

weeks with the Rangers there were two lonely letters in the slot. I wasn't insulted, but it didn't seem right. Did people know I'd been traded? Was my slot in Cincinnati still full?

I decided to ask the clubbie. I tried to be cool about it, so I grabbed the two or three letters out of my slot and said, "Geez, I guess everybody's forgotten about me."

He looked at me like I was stupid. When he realized I wasn't kidding, he raised his eyebrows and laughed.

"Really?" he said. "You think they've forgotten about you?"

With that, he pointed to the ceiling.

I don't know why I hadn't noticed, but sitting on the shelf high above the mail slots there were large mail crates. There were four of them, and the one with the most mail flowing over the sides was marked HAMILTON.

"Oh, man—there they are," I said.

Now I did feel stupid.

"Yeah," he said. "There's the mail for the forgotten man."

■ ■ ■

A new team meant new interest. I got together with the Rangers' media-relations staff to plan a spring training press conference that would make it easier on everyone. Instead of having to tell my story every day, I preferred to do it once for all the local media and anybody else who might have interest. That way, the television stations could get everything they needed on tape, for use now and in the future.

Of course, I knew it wouldn't work out that way, because I wouldn't turn anyone down who arrived at my locker asking me to discuss my story. So many national reporters travel through spring training, and even though it can become a chore to rehash every aspect of my downfall and recovery, I do it for a couple of reasons. First, as I've said, it really serves as therapy for me to stand up in front of a group of people and tell my story. It reinforces the decision to stay clean and sober, and as I'm talking I imagine all those people out there—those who have had addiction problems and those who haven't, kids and parents alike—who might be helped by hearing what I've gone through and how I've changed my life.

Second, I'm an employee of the team and part of my job is to talk to the media to reach the fans to tell them about our team.

The press conference was routine, with all the usual questions about the types of drugs I used, coupled with the quizzical looks on their faces. I'd recognize that look anywhere, the look that asks the question, "How in the world could you have done that to yourself?"

Some of the reporters, typically and understandably, wanted to know the salacious details of my drug use. Not only which drugs, but how often and how much. Their strategy is to push till I push back, maybe as a sort of test, but I haven't pushed back yet. I'm fine with the scrutiny; it comes with the territory.

But at some point during the press conference, I looked to the back of the room, past the reporters in their seats and the television cameras on their tripods, to see three people sitting in folding chairs. In street clothes, there were three of my new teammates—second baseman Ian Kinsler, shortstop Michael Young, and third baseman Hank Blalock.

These were the three faces of the franchise, leaders on the field and in the clubhouse. At some point, the reporters noticed them as well, and one of them asked me a series of questions.

"Josh, how many of these press conferences would you say you've done?"

"A lot."

"Have you ever had teammates show up to support you?"

I was a little bit confused by the question. I said, "No," kind of hesitantly, because that was the truth. With the Reds, I gave a press conference much like this one during spring training and I followed it by giving one at the beginning of every series on the road, to allow the local reporters to all ask their questions and get their stories before the first game.

With the Reds, none of my teammates had attended any of those sessions, but I never thought anything of it. I never expected them to sit there and listen to me tell my story for the millionth time.

And in this case, it never occurred to me that Ian, Michael, and Hank were there to support me. I just assumed they were having their own press conferences after mine, so when I saw them back there I figured they were waiting for me to hurry up and get it over with.

Once I heard the question and understood why they were there, I didn't know what to say. I looked at them and felt tears welling up. This was a touching moment. I'd become accustomed to being somewhat of a loner in my life, set apart by the circumstances that forced me to set myself apart. But this felt like togetherness. This felt like a team. These guys were interested in hearing my story so they could better understand what I've gone through and the battle I still fight. More than anything, I was humbled by their presence.

I've always been self-conscious about my position. I never doubt my ability to play at this level, but the attention I've received because of my story has been both wonderful and troublesome. It had its downside in Cincinnati. I don't want to be separate from my teammates, but my life has made some separation inevitable. I walk a fine line, and it nearly took my breath away to see the best and most established players on my new team show that kind of compassion and understanding.

The next week, after an afternoon workout, Kinsler asked me if I wanted to go get some dinner. Not a big deal, right? Well, it was the first time a teammate had ever asked me to do something away from the ballpark since I had come to the big leagues.

The guys in Cincinnati were probably afraid that I would say no, or that I couldn't go somewhere alcohol was served. Maybe it was because Johnny was always around, or maybe they didn't want to invite me somewhere and then feel like they couldn't order a beer in my presence.

Kinsler and I started hanging out. His spring training condo was right below mine, and he roomed with his wife and first baseman Jason Botts. We would wind down after a day of practice by playing Halo 3 or watching a hunting show on television.

This carried into the regular season. I went to movies with Kinsler. Milton Bradley would call after we got back to the hotel after a night game on the road and plan breakfast the next morning.

The good vibes carried onto the field. We started the season poorly—at one point we were 9–17 and it seemed our manager, Ron Washington, was going to lose his job—but we rebounded to get ourselves over .500. Our pitching was inconsistent, but our offense was the best in the majors. With Ian and Michael getting on base for me and Milton, we made it uncomfortable for every pitcher we faced. I led the league in RBIs from the beginning of the season, and I had so many—95 at the All-Star break—that it became a joke between Milton and me. He hit behind me in the lineup and kept complaining, in a friendly way, that he couldn't get any RBIs because by the time he got to the plate I'd already driven them in.

Starting in mid-May, I started climbing the ladder in the All-Star voting. The team pushed for Rangers fans to vote, and before long it developed its own momentum. By mid-June it was pretty clear I would be voted one of the three starting outfielders for the American League, and by the time voting closed I had passed Manny Ramirez of the Red Sox to become the leading vote-getter among American League outfielders. The other three guys at the top of our batting order—Ian, Michael, and Milton— also were named to the team.

I felt like part of the team in Cincinnati, and I believe God put me there for a reason to start my career in a baseball-crazed city. But from the moment Ian, Michael, and Hank sat down in the back of the room during my spring training press conference, I felt at home with the Rangers. It just felt right, like this, too, was meant to be.

TWENTY

I MADE A DECISION early in my recovery that I couldn't rehabilitate my soul without complete honesty. My decisions were my decisions. The easiest path would have been to blame someone else, or blame circumstances, or blame fate. Had I done that, had I avoided responsibility and shifted blame, I wouldn't be where I am today.

I went from being a can't-miss prospect, a young man praised for my ability on the ballfield and my attitude off it, to being an aimless, nearly hopeless drug addict. I went from being an eighteen-year-old whose talent was worth $3.96 million to the Tampa Bay Devil Rays two days after I finished high school to being the kind of man who would hand over his wife's wedding ring to a drug dealer for crack. I went from being a respectful young man who kissed his grandmother before every game to being the kind of man whose sole purpose in life was to acquire and use substances that would damage me and my relationships with the people I loved.

How did it happen? Easy question, tough answer. My journey to the depths of human depravity—to a place where a single-minded desire to alter my consciousness was my only goal—defies logic.

Equally illogical is my return journey, back to becoming a responsible man. I wake up every morning striving to be the best husband, father, and baseball player I can be that day. I take nothing for granted. In my life, one day at a time is not a cliché, it is a necessity.

None of this would have been possible without my relationship with Christ. I went through eight different drug treatment and rehabilitation clinics, but my personal resurrection did not come from a group session or a therapist's couch. I know the twelve steps by heart, but my healing did not come from a strict adherence to those principles. Instead, my life changed from hopeless to hope-filled when I turned to God and asked for His help. I recognized my failings and, most important, my inability to heal myself.

I know not everybody believes the way I do, but I can only document my journey. I can only tell my story, and I believe there would be no story without faith. The ultimate destination for this journey would be vastly different without my faith in Jesus. What would that destination be? Given the path I was on, it's hard to imagine I would be alive right now, much less alive and writing a book that I hope can educate and inspire. You might still be reading a book about Josh Hamilton if I had not turned my life over to Jesus Christ, but that book would be written by someone else, and it would most likely be a tragedy.

My story is three parts inspiration, one part warning.

I was humbled twice, once by addiction and again by recovery.

I'll end with a story: In May 2007, after a night game during a homestand while I was a Red, Katie and the girls loaded into the truck in the players' parking lot at Great American Ballpark. I was tired, we had just lost another game during a bad stretch, and all I wanted to do was get home and get some sleep.

Getting into the truck and leaving the ballpark are two different things, though. Win or lose, good game or bad, there's always a group of fans standing outside the entrance to the parking lot, looking for autographs. I always try to stop and sign as many as is reasonable.

Signing my name is not a big deal, no matter how tired I am. You never know whose life you might touch, or whose might touch yours.

Among those waiting on this night was a boy of about nine or ten wearing a Reds cap and an imploring, hopeful look. None of this was in any way unusual, but when he came up to the side of the truck and handed me a baseball to sign, he said, "Josh, you're my savior."

I looked up from the signing to look at him. His eyes were big and honest, and he was so sincere I can still close my eyes and see them today.

"Well, thank you," I said. "Do you know who my savior is?"

He thought for a minute. I could see the gears turning. Finally, he blurted out "Jesus Christ!" like he just came up with the answer to a test.

"That's exactly right," I said.

I slapped him five, signed for a few more people, and left the parking lot. The little boy stuck with me, though, and with Katie. There was something so heartfelt and passionate in his demeanor, something that was both innocent and pleading.

Maybe Katie and I understood there was something deeper at work in that little boy, that maybe he was sent to teach us another lesson on how God works through us. Our encounter with him touched me so much that I told it for a story in *ESPN The Magazine* about two months later. And shortly after that, I received a letter from the boy's aunt; she had read the magazine article and wanted me to know a little more of the story.

The letter explained that the boy's father was an alcoholic who had struggled repeatedly trying to get sober. The boy and his father were huge Reds fans, and the boy followed my story closely. The boy brought up my story with his dad, and they had discussed my recovery and what an inspiration it was to a lot of people.

According to the letter, the boy's father told him he was going to use my example to try to get clean. They were working together, with the little boy telling his dad he could do if I could do it. At the time the letter was written, the boy's dad had put together an impressive stretch of sobriety.

I got chills as I read the letter. I handed it to Katie, and she teared up as she read it. We looked at each other with the exact same look we had shared the night we drove out of the parking lot after talking to that boy. She just smiled and shook her head. We didn't have to say a word, but we were thinking the exact same thing: *This is about so much more than baseball.*

EPILOGUE

THE ALL-STAR GAME is always a major production, baseball's midseason showcase, but the 2008 All-Star Game at Yankee Stadium was intended to make all others shrink in comparison. Everything that happens in New York is bigger than life, but an All-Star Game in the final season of historic Yankee Stadium? It didn't need exaggeration.

About three weeks before the game, I got a call from a representative for Major League Baseball, asking me if I would participate in the Home Run Derby the day before the game. I asked no questions and didn't hesitate. "You bet I will," I said.

I thought back to the dream I had at the Winning Inning, when I was competing in the Home Run Derby and telling a female reporter—and, by extension, the world—how the Lord saved my life and brought me to this moment.

One of the first calls I made was to Clay Council, the old coach from Cary American Legion. I had a promise to keep.

"Hey, Clay, what are you doing right now?"

"I'm fixing to head down to Athens Drive High to throw to some boys," he said.

"Well, how would you like to throw to me in the Home

Run Derby, in front of fifty-five thousand people at Yankee Stadium?"

"I think I'd like that," he said.

"Now, tell me—you're not going to tighten up on me,
are you?"

"No," he said, seeming to think about it some. "I won't
tighten up, but I might have a heart attack."

Clay was seventy-one years old, but I knew he could
still throw. I hit off him maybe fifteen times before, but
one of those came during the past off-season. He was as
good as anybody who threw in the big leagues.

Still, this was different. This was a bigger stage than
either of us had ever experienced.

Before I hung up, I told Clay, "Don't worry about it;
it'll be fun."

Major League Baseball paid for Clay's flight to New
York, and he took the same flight as Katie and the girls.
They needed to make a uniform for him, and when they
asked me to spell his name I thought I knew. I told them,
"C-O-U-N-S-I-L." Spelling was never my best subject,
and I guess I should have asked.

And that's why Clay wore a jersey with his name mis-
spelled during his big moment at the Home Run Derby.

■ ■ ■

In the moments leading up to the derby, Clay and I went
into the tunnel leading from the clubhouse to the home
dugout. We could hear the rumble of the crowd rattling
above us. We bowed our heads and prayed.

I said, "Lord, thank you for the opportunity and the
platform to spread Your word and glorify You."

I was the last hitter of the first round, and the crowd

was loud from the second I stepped into the batter's box. After my second homer was announced at 502 feet, my teammate Ian Kinsler came over to wipe my face with a towel as the roar from the crowd swelled. I said, "That's only two," and held up two fingers, but it didn't matter. It seemed as if everybody sensed something special was going to happen even before it did.

The noise was ridiculous. It felt like I was standing in a bowl and the roar of the crowd was coming down on me like thunder. I'd never heard anything like it. As I stepped in after my second homer, I looked at the catcher and said, "Man, this is awesome."

Once I got into a rhythm, once the shots started carrying higher and farther, it felt unreal. Clay was hitting the right spots and I was connecting with the fat part of the bat on every swing. I squared up one after another—12, 13, 14, 15.

My teammates said it was no real surprise to them. When Michael Young was interviewed during my round, he said he'd been watching the same thing through the entire first half of the season.

I took a deep breath. I turned and looked into the stands to find my family. Katie was there, more than seven months pregnant. Sierra and Julia were there. My parents were there, as were Katie's parents. I invited Granny, but at seventy-eight years old, the idea of fighting New York City and Yankee Stadium was a little too much for her. Besides, she felt she could see better if she stayed home and watched it on television. "That way I can see your face," she told me.

What did I see when I looked up into the stands? My dad's smile was like a row of lights coming at me. Katie was just laughing her head off—no tears, just pure happiness.

This had a different feel to it. Unlike my first Opening Day or so many other moments during my rookie season, this moment didn't carry any of the emotion from the past.

This was a celebration of right now, about what I had become and not what I had been. It felt good.

And the guys on the field, from both the American and National leagues, were reacting like they'd never seen anything like it.

The hardest part about this was keeping calm and composed under the circumstances. I told myself it wasn't any different from what I'd been doing my entire life, from hitting with my older brother's Legion team to hitting with Jose Canseco the day I signed, to hitting at the Winning Inning with Katie watching for the first time.

But it was different. This was the most bloated, exaggerated version of batting practice anybody could ever imagine. Instead of a few people showing up to watch, there were fifty-five thousand. Instead of an opposing team sneaking looks during stretching and talking under their breath, there were two All-Star teams—the best players on the planet—sitting there expecting a show, watching and responding openly to every pitch. Not to mention the millions of people watching on television.

There was a little bit of pressure.

I had looked at the field earlier that day and saw a small section where the upper deck gives way to the bleachers in right center, and I told some reporters I thought there was a chance I could hit one in that little sliver and it would carry all the way out of the stadium and into the New York night.

I don't think they believed me, but when I hit one 504 feet into the third deck in right field, just a few feet away from finding that spot, they might have reconsidered.

At one point I hit thirteen straight pitches over the

fence. I finished with 28 homers in the first round, beating Bobby Abreu's old single-round record by four. Nobody else hit more than 8. After homer number 28, Milton Bradley ran over to me, put his arm around me, and raised his cell phone to take a picture of the two of us. At some point, probably around homer number 15, I became aware of a chant rolling through the stands.

"Ham-il-ton. Ham-il-ton. Ham-il-ton."

Oh, man, I thought, this is getting crazy. The fans in Yankee Stadium are chanting my name? This didn't even happen in my dream.

Rewind to two weeks previous, when we were in New York to play the Yankees. I was standing in center field when a chant broke out in the outfield bleachers:

"Josh smokes crack."

"Josh smokes crack."

Over and over, droning on and on.

Josh. Smokes. Crack.

Josh. Smokes. Crack.

In a way, their chants were a pretty good summary of how far I had traveled.

Let the Yankee Stadium crowd tell the story:

From "Josh smokes crack" to "Ham-il-ton."

■ ■ ■

In my dream, I finished hitting and spoke to a female reporter. In reality, on July 14, 2008, in Yankee Stadium, I finished hitting and was met by Erin Andrews of ESPN.

Have I mentioned I don't believe in coincidence?

She talked to me about the dream and asked me if the dream could compare to the reality. I told her, "Well, in the dream I didn't know how many I hit."

She asked Clay to describe his feelings, and he pointed to me and said, "I made the All-Star team and got only one vote—his."

Clay and I were both a little worn out from the first round. He threw fifty-four pitches, and I put everything I had into those swings. As Erin Andrews was walking away, the microphones caught Clay asking me, "You mean we got to go again?"

I went up against Justin Morneau in the finals, and he beat me, 5–3. It didn't matter that I hit more in the competition than he did, and it really didn't matter to me that I didn't win. Once again, I went back to the dream I had at the Winning Inning: The reason I didn't know how many homers I hit in the dream was that God didn't care. I was able to use the platform to glorify Him and spread my story.

You can't put a score on that.

■ ■ ■

Katie woke up the next morning in our hotel room and asked, "Did I dream that, or did it really happen?" I turned on the television and flipped to ESPN, where they were showing a replay.

"Nope, looks real," I said.

Later that morning I was reminded that my life hadn't changed completely. There was a knock on the door of my hotel room, and standing there was a pee tester with his briefcase-sized kit in his hand.

He identified himself and came in. It sounds kind of corny, but I was watching *The Natural* on television when he showed up. It was almost over, so I asked him if I could wait until it ended to take care of business.

He said he didn't mind, so we sat there on the edge of the bed, me and the pee-test guy, watching *The Natural*.

■ ■ ■

The attention that came my way after the All-Star Game was heartwarming, and a little intimidating. It was the highest-rated Home Run Derby ever, and everyone who watched heard my story over and over. (Not all of what was reported on television was accurate, however; for one thing, I never once used heroin, let alone became a heroin addict.)

Katie and the girls flew back to Raleigh with Clay, and when they walked through the airport people recognized Clay and started asking for his autograph. He didn't expect that, and he didn't expect to get the official All-Star ring—the same ones they give the players—that I bought him to thank him for helping me out.

The irony wasn't lost on me. Here I was buying someone a ring as a memento of a good time; before, I was selling or bartering rings to get drugs.

Our second series after the break was in Chicago, and when the bus pulled up outside the Westin on North Michigan Avenue on Sunday evening, at least one hundred people stood outside the doors calling out to me.

That night, I went to a movie. I stood in line to buy popcorn and ended up posing for pictures for more than ten minutes.

And before the first game of that series, I had a man come up to me while I was signing autographs and say, "Josh, I brought my sister here to see you."

The woman, probably in her thirties, stood there smiling but not looking happy.

"My sister can't get off drugs," the man said. "She's tried everything."

The woman said, "I want to stop, but I just can't."

Think about this for a moment. This man brought his sister to a Major League Baseball game on a Monday night to seek help for her drug habit from a ballplayer neither of them had ever met. She had come willingly, setting aside any shame she might have felt in being identified as a drug user in a public setting. They had no guarantee that I would even see them at the game, much less be in a position where I could speak to them. But here we were, in a crowd of people jostling for position to talk about the Home Run Derby and get my autograph, having a deep discussion about life and death.

"When you really want to change your life, you will," I told her. "Something is going to have to happen in your life for you to get better. You're going to hit bottom — maybe get arrested, maybe OD. But when you go to meetings, the first thing they talk about is a higher power. They talk about God, and the only way I was able to get better is through Jesus Christ."

They nodded and thanked me. I signed a ball for her and wrote "James 4:7" under my signature. I wished her luck and said a prayer in my mind for her. There are so many people out there searching. So many people who struggle and want to do better but can't find the strength. So many confused, sad, desperate people who need the right kind of guidance to change their lives.

People just like me.

ABOUT THE
AUTHORS

JOSH HAMILTON is an All-Star outfielder for the Texas Rangers. A native of Raleigh, North Carolina, he lives in Apex, North Carolina, with his wife, Katie, and their three daughters.

TIM KEOWN is a senior writer for *ESPN The Magazine*. He is the author of *Skyline: One Season, One Team, One City,* and the coauthor of *Bad As I Wanna Be* (with Dennis Rodman) and *Hunting the Jackal* (with Billy Waugh). He lives in Northern California with his wife, Miriam, and their four sons.